ARTHRITIS BEATEN TODAY!

D1350497

Dr L Sands

ARTHRITIS BEATEN TODAY!

2nd Edition
Copyright 2001 by L. Sands

ALL RIGHTS RESERVED

Published by

Vectropy Publishing

an imprint of Beckett Karlson

The Studio, Denton, Peterborough PE7 3SD

Need to know more? Call free in UK: 0800 0182 082

and +44 1733 310910 (overseas)

Foreword

When one has tried and failed with so many remedies for arthritis, anything new that comes along is bound to be met with skepticism. I saw my father's arthritis advance to a distressing degree. He had already reached the point where walking was a painful chore, and we both dreaded the progressively crippling future that was in store for him. As a physician, it was doubly frustrating for me.

Even when my highly respected colleague, Dr. Sands, told me about the phenomenal results he was getting with arthritis patients from his new project, I was still a bit sceptical. After all, when something sounds too good to be true, it usually is. For his researchers to have found a substance that permanently reverses the arthritic process with just one set of capsules was practically unbelievable. And for that substance to be totally free of harmful side effects was just too much to ask.

Yet, in just a few days, I saw all signs of my father's arthritis completely disappear. He is now just as active as he was before his arthritis ever struck. Believe me, he is a man of great energy and it seems a miracle to see him striding around again as he had done so many years before. He has now been totally free of arthritis for over six months without the need for further treatment of any kind.

Dr. Sands tells me that his greatest obstacle in presenting this substance, CMO, to the world lies in over-coming the skepticism of the public and the medical profession as well. I can understand that for I, too, initially had my doubts. But thank God, I felt it was worth a try and my father is a spry and active man again.

F. A. Muñoz, MD

A Message From the Author

In the few years since my first CMO book was published I have seen CMO become an international phenomenon. It is now available on every continent of the world and it has made a tremendous impact on 100,000's of people who had been suffering from arthritis. The joy this brings to my heart is immeasurable.

And we have also discovered through experience that CMO is helping to control and sometimes, even curing, virtually any ailment with autoimmune components or chronic inflammatory factors.

Our experiences have also taught us a great deal about autoimmune processes and how easily they can be triggered. There are new chapters in this book that suggest ways to deal with that problem.

Dr. L. Sands, ND, Ph.D.

Contents

Introduction

Information Vital to the Understanding of this Book

INTRODUCTION

CMO. Call it what you will: rescue, remission, relief, reversal, intervention, or cure - thousands who had suffered for years and years with arthritis, and have now experienced its total disappearance, call it a miracle.

Instead of popping pills or taking shots day after day or hour after hour merely to get some sort of temporary relief from their symptoms, they found that just one course of capsules eliminated their ailment completely - without the need for further remedies of any kind.

Imagine never needing to take another pill or shot ever again for your arthritis!

All that from a simple substance naturally derived from certain fatty tissue of beef and put in capsule form: cerasomal-cis-9-cetylmyristoleate. It bears the registered trade name of CMO. It is a rare but natural substance. We're certain you even eat some from time to time. Minute trace amounts of it are commonly found in butter and products made with butter. But as a healer of autoimmune ailments, there's never been anything like it before, especially for arthritis. Nothing in this world has even come close to the results obtained from CMO. That's what this book is all about.

But first let's talk about a book that talks about a cure that isn't a cure at all.

The "Arthritis Cure" that isn't

The so-called "medical miracle" described in the recently touted book, *The Arthritis Cure*, published by St. Martins Press, has been justifiably disputed by most well-informed medical professionals. Let us go on record, clearly and unequivocally, that the treatments described in that book certainly are not a cure for arthritis any more than aspirin is a cure for arthritis.

Although the use of glucosamines and chondroitins urged by the book can often produce good short-term effects, it has rarely shown any long-lasting value. That's because glucosamines and chondroitins are merely the building blocks for the body to construct new cartilage. They help the body produce replacement cartilage at a faster rate, but they do nothing to stop the destruction of the arthritic process itself. The best one can hope for is to temporarily replace cartilage as fast as, or possibly even a little faster than it's being destroyed. But usually, and inevitably, the destruction outpaces the repair and arthritis continues to worsen. That's no "cure"!

Even the Arthritis Foundation has, in its news release of 15 January 1997, stated, *"The Arthritis Cure* [book] is not recommended."* The release also states, "The Arthritis Foundation cannot recommend glucosamine and chondroitin sulfate as a treatment for osteoarthritis or any other form of arthritis."

Nevertheless, the book has a great deal of merit. Its glucosamine-chondroitin therapy is far better than using methotrexate, cortisones, pain killers, or anti-inflammatory drugs. Those can relieve some of the bothersome symptoms of arthritis but they won't help the joints in any way. By masking the pain, those drugs could readily encourage the abuse of an already damaged joint and hasten its way to total destruction.

The REAL Arthritis Cure

Nevertheless, the arthritic process can be halted. Arthritis can be reversed. The pain and inflammation can be relieved. And it's all been done without any harmful side effects. That's right, it has already been done for thousands of arthritis sufferers, and the substance that's done it is available to you right now! It's called CMO.

In their October 28, 1996 issue, *TIME* magazine reported on the three most promising developments in arthritis research. The scientists participating in all three projects are intensely focussed on intervening in the immune system's involvement in the arthritic process. But it will be several years before the results of these investigations will trickle down to be of any benefit for the public. It may be years before you even hear of it again.

This book reports on a substance discovered years ago by a researcher at a U.S. Government National Institutes of Health (NIH) research facility. It is already available now and has already succeeded in that magical immunological intervention for thousands of extremely grateful ex-arthritic individuals.

Furthermore, its benefits appear to last indefinitely, probably eliminating the need for any additional arthritis medication ever again. The active ingredient is derived from natural fatty beef tissue. This natural compound bears the rather long and complicated bioscientific name of cerasomal-cis-9-cetylmyristoleate. But it's best known by its commercial name of CMO - a lot easier to remember and pronounce. For that reason it will, henceforth, be referred to as CMO in the rest of the book.

Dr. Douglas Hunt (MD) has written, "CMO will probably be seen as the most important find of the twentieth century." He goes on to say, "And it does its job with a few ... capsules of powder. Many who've taken CMO have been free of rheumatoid arthritis for as long as nine years."

Mindful of its safety and immediate availability, CMO certainly warrants consideration as an option for anyone with rheumatoid arthritis, osteoarthritis, and virtually all types of arthritic manifestations other than that of gout.

This valuable and responsible book was prepared by staff members of the San Diego Clinic, the facility which continued the exploration of CMO that started at the NIH so many years ago. This clinic prepared the model for the first extended professional study of CMO encompassing several dozen individual subjects. It is also the major communications centre receiving daily reports from numerous medical practitioners and arthritis victims around the country who are currently using CMO. Thus, this book contains the most valuable and most recent of all information from medical professionals, patients, and consumers on the results of CMO in practical day-to-day use. It also includes a great many exciting case histories and personal reports.

It also tells the story of the development of CMO - from the discovery of its basic precursor at the NIH to the evolution of the final modern product available today. It includes dozens of up-close and personal stories - even reports of how CMO has rescued people who had already been told by their doctors that they should prepare for imminent death. It also reports on those previously confined to wheelchairs who have returned to a normal happy lifestyle. Of course these are the more extreme cases, but even the average cases are quite dramatic, especially for the people themselves who have regained the use of their hands, or who can now walk again comfortably, or even for those who are simply no longer wracked with pain every single day.

The book also relates how swindlers are preying on the public by producing, would you believe, worthless counterfeit CMO! It's an amazing and enlightening book for all to read. It's an absolute must for anyone who has, or knows someone who has, any form of arthritis.

Please share this book with your family, friends, and neighbours. You can be sure they'll thank you for it.

Chapter One

A Briefing on the Arthritic Process

A Briefing on
the Arthritic Process

The *TIME* magazine article referred to in the Introduction of this book begins like this: "A KILLER WAS ON THE LOOSE ... It was her own immune system, which had gone berserk, attacking the joints in her body and crippling her so badly that she often had to use a wheelchair. Left unchecked, rheumatoid arthritis might have shortened her life 10 to 15 years."

The article reports on how all three of the most advanced scientific research projects today are intensely focussed on intervening in the immune system involvement in the arthritic process.

Of course the first thing you probably want to know is how any of this, including this book, can benefit you personally - specifically, how you, like the thousands before you, can be rescued from the crippling pain and inflammation of arthritis. First, it's important for you to know a bit about the arthritic process in order to understand how it can be reversed.

Stopping the symptoms doesn't stop the disease

There have been thousands of volumes written by thousands of authors on the how-and-why theories of arthritis. There are almost as many different theories as there are authors. Some of them are pretty screwy, but all of them are pretty scary.

The scary part is that no one has been able to stop the relentless, destructive advance of arthritis - until now!

Sure, you may sometimes slow it down a bit through diet and nutritional supplements. You can ease the symptoms with anti-inflammatory drugs and pain relievers. Your doctor can clobber your system with highly toxic anti-cancer drugs like

Methotrexate (also disguised under the less frightening name of Rheumatrex), which just maybe could give you some temporary relief at the cost of sacrificing your liver. But, until now, nobody has been able to halt the destructive onslaught against your cartilage and your joints.

How does the arthritic process start?

TIME magazine gives this elegantly simple answer: "The problem starts when, for reasons no one fully understands, a few misguided T-cells incite other immune system cells called macrophages to attack the joints."

Those so-called "misguided T-cells" are actually what are known as memory T-cells. In the arthritic process (whether rheumatoid, osteo, or other) these memory T-cells develop an internal program, just like some sort of computer, which commands macrophage cells to attack and destroy cartilage. This destructive process results in the inflammation of the joints that is so typical in people afflicted with the disease.

The inflammation, in turn, affects the nerves and that's what usually causes the associated pain. The inflammation may also push some bones out of place resulting in the disfigurement that is so typically found in arthritic joints.

Unfortunately, those memory T-cells never give up. It seems their malfunctioning programs go on forever. Moreover, they clone themselves, generating more and more misprogrammed T-cells that direct more and more attacks against your cartilage. That's why, as time passes, arthritis only gets worse, virtually never gets better.

But how does it all start? No one is absolutely certain, but probably it's because some macrophages discover some particles of diseased or damaged cartilage that needs to be disposed of.

Macrophages are like garbage collectors inside your body. Their job is to get rid of any foreign matter and organisms they encounter. They destroy invading organisms like viruses and bacteria, and they clean up waste matter as well. That includes any fragments of unhealthy cartilage damaged by some physical trauma or produced by some invading organism like that which causes rheumatic fever - or maybe even the flu. (Remember those achy feelings in your joints when you had a serious bout with the flu?).

Why does it keep getting worse?

In the case of arthritis, once macrophages have dealt with some particles of cartilage they develop a chemical message that's passed on to the memory T-cells. If there's only one message of that type, the memory T-cells ignore it, but if that message is repeated then they develop a program instructing more and more macrophages to dispose of the cartilage. Unfortunately, that message doesn't (or maybe can't) distinguish between healthy or unhealthy cartilage. So the destructive onslaught against your joints begins.

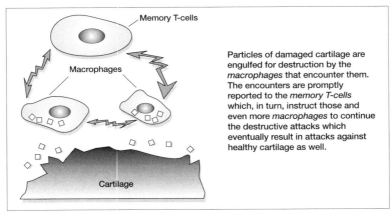

Memory T-cells

Macrophages

Cartilage

Particles of damaged cartilage are engulfed for destruction by the *macrophages* that encounter them. The encounters are promptly reported to the *memory T-cells* which, in turn, instruct those and even more *macrophages* to continue the destructive attacks which eventually result in attacks against healthy cartilage as well.

It seems that it is the inflammatory process itself that initiates the arthritic process, regardless of what triggers the inflammation. In other words, the arthritic process can start whether the particles of cartilage result from an attack by certain pathogenic micro-organisms (leading to rheumatoid arthritis) or by a trauma (developing into osteoarthritis)!

In either case, rheumatoid or osteoarthritis, it results in a vicious cycle. As more macrophages bring back messages to the memory T-cells, more and more T-cells develop programs that direct attacks against the cartilage and arthritis continues to get progressively worse. You almost never hear of arthritis getting better. Now you've learned why.

Isn't there some way to stop this destructive Autoimmune system process?

Now what if you could get in there and somehow intervene or interrupt that vicious chain of events? Shouldn't that halt the arthritic process, stopping it dead in its tracks? Absolutely - regardless of whether it's rheumatoid or osteoarthritis! However, there are no conventional pharmaceuticals that can safely alter the process that is causing the attacks against your cartilage. Nevertheless, quite fortunately, Mother Nature has provided one. We'll get to that shortly.

TIME reports that one of the three pharmaceutical companies researching more creative approaches to the treatment of arthritis is working on a custom-made antibody that "can temporarily knock the immune cells out of commission." The company claims that more than half of the 122 patients in one study showed "significant improvement without debilitating side effects." That is further confirmation that intervening in the autoimmune process can affect the arthritic cycle. The *TIME* article also concludes that none of the three drugs being studied can cure the disease: "When patients stop taking them, pain and stiffness return."

Well, that certainly indicates some progress, but it was only a study and it's going to take several years before anything trickles down to where something may become available to the public. When it does, it will prove to be prohibitively expensive for almost all but the wealthy or the fully insured. Furthermore, it may be years before you even hear of it again. And the side effects may be horrific.

Fortunately there's no need to wait for help. Decades ago a researcher employed at the US National Institutes of Health discovered a substance that does all that the most advanced researchers today dare hope to accomplish - *and more!* The modern evolution of that substance is called CMO. And yes, it does interrupt the cycle of events and put a halt to the arthritic process with no harmful side effects. Furthermore, reports over the years indicate the benefits seem to be permanent. And it's a product derived from purely natural sources. (Mother Nature triumphs again!).

Where has it been hiding all these years? The mystery shall unfold in the chapters that follow - along with full details of how it's made, where it comes from, and how it evolved into a modern day miracle against arthritis. But first, it will be useful for you to learn additional information about the underlying autoimmune system processes that cause arthritis in the first place.

Understanding the Autoimmune Process

In the beginning of this chapter we explained the arthritic process. Now it might be useful to explain autoimmune processes in genera] with greater clarity. A keen understanding can be very useful in everyday life. Let's start with a simple step-by-step explanation of the arthritic process because that applies to virtually every human autoimmune process and virtually all diseases with autoimmune factors.

The Autoimmune-Arthritic Process - Step-By-Step

The following is an overview of the autoimmune-arthritic process. The process is explained in eleven steps. It all starts with initiation of altered autoimmune system function.

1.   First, infection, trauma, or excessive wear affects the joints. The usual infections are rheumatic fever, flu, or bacteria. Traumas include events such as, jolts or injuries from auto wrecks, falls, sports injuries, jogging, etc. Excessive joint wear comes from being overweight, or from repetitive use of keyboards, jackhammers, knitting needles, screwdrivers etc.

2.   The effects of #1 cause damaged or infected cartilage particles to be dislodged from their normal site. This happens regardless of whether it's rheumatoid, reactive, or osteoarthritis.

3.   Macrophages of the immune system begin a cleanup of these dislodged cartilage particles. That's a normal part of their job.

4.   Macrophages report their activities to dormant memory T-cells, which are the commanding "generals" of the immune system that direct the activities of other immune cells.

5.   The reports from the macrophages activate the dormant memory T-cells, then develop aggressive anti-cartilage cleanup programs. Unfortunately, these programs do not distinguish between healthy and damaged cartilage.

6.   The memory T-cell programs stimulate more macrophage activity which, in turn, activates even more dormant memory T-cells.

21

7. The increased memory T-cell population continues to stimulate more macrophage activity, and the self-perpetuating cycle of cartilage destruction expands. Because the memory T-cell programs don't limit macrophage activity to damaged cartilage only, destruction of healthy cartilage also occurs. It has now developed into a destructive autoimmune process. But, until sufficient cartilage has been destroyed, symptoms are not evident. The individual is unaware that the destructive process is occurring .

8. The initiating factor (infection, trauma, weight) taking place in #1, may have disappeared many months or years ago, but the destructive autoimmune process remains active. It is self perpetuating and no longer dependent upon the initiating factor. When this happens it has become a pure autoimmune disease.

9. The cycle is compounded by the fact that the mechanism which should deactivate certain memory T-cells (those that have completed their mission) fails to function. The constant macrophage re-stimulation of the memory T-cells keeps them active. The memory T-cells also re-stimulate each other. So now there is an overabundance of memory T-cells propelling macrophage cartilage destruction. The immune system is now totally out of control and massive cartilage destruction often begins. Early symptoms of pain and inflammation often appear.

10. Cartilage destruction accelerates. The cycle reaches an explosive critical mass. Macrophages are now scouring the body to find and destroy any cartilage anywhere it can be found. Symptoms become more severe. Pain, inflammation, and joint deformity intensify at old sites and now appear at new sites as they suffer macrophage attacks. Any or all joints may be affected, including the spine.

11. Symptoms of pain, stiffness, swelling, nodules, and deformation often reach intolerable and crippling levels - especially as joint cartilage disappears and bone-on-bone erosion occurs. Conventional arthritis medications also take their toll on the liver, kidneys, and heart. Normal life span is often shortened by ten or twenty years not only from the ravages of arthritis, but from the side effects of both prescription and over-the-counter medications as well.

By deactivating the memory T-cells, CMO intervention (the sooner the better) can stop the autoimmune process at any point.

Current medical dogma holds that only rheumatoid arthritis is an autoimmune disease. On the contrary, the above explanation makes it evident that osteoarthritis is an autoimmune disease as well. The sooner the medical community accepts that fact, the better they may be able to treat their arthritis patients effectively.

Autoimmune factors in other diseases

It is important to note that this very same process occurs with virtually all diseases that have autoimmune factors. It is often the crippling factor in neurological diseases like multiple sclerosis, Alzheimer's, Parkinson's, ALS, polyneuropathy, and other demyelinating diseases. In these diseases, instead of cartilage it is nerve or brain tissue that is being attacked and destroyed through the autoimmune process.

Chronic inflammatory processes such as those found in fibromyalgia, emphysema, lupus, Crohn's disease, diverticulitis, irritable bowel syndrome, colitis, tendinitis, and many other ailments are also the result of faulty or detrimental autoimmune regulation. Autoimmune factors also play a role in diseases like myasthenia gravis, muscular dystrophy, cerebral palsy, post polio syndrome, Grave's disease, autism, attention deficit disorder, asthma, allergy, and many others.

It has also been recently discovered that chronic inflammatory processes play a very significant role in many cardiovascular attacks and diseases. The value of CMO for the prevention and treatment of these diseases is discussed in another chapter of this book.

CMO is an adaptogenic immunomodulator

From our work we have found that only CMO has corrective and restorative immunomodulatory properties for autoimmune diseases. Other so-called "immunomodulators" do not. They function primarily as immunosuppressants or immunostimulants. They are capable of only one principal action, either suppressing or stimulating immune function.

CMO, on the other hand, *corrects* autoimmune programs within the memory T-cells themselves rather than just *temporarily* suppressing or stimulating immune system activities. That is why a single CMO therapy program can correct memory T-cell faults without any need to continually apply the therapy or use any additional medication of any kind.

CMO is not an immunosuppressant, nor an immunostimulant. Nor is it a pharmaceutical. It is a naturally derived substance. Some practitioners have speculated that, in the case of arthritis for example, CMO merely acts upon pain receptors at the arthritic site. If that were so, CMO's effects would not be so permanent. Furthermore, that theory cannot explain:

- how CMO lowers blood sedimentation rates in lupus patients,
- or how it reverses lung inflammation in emphysema,

- or how it lowers the need for insulin in diabetics,
- or how it reverses prostate inflammation,
- or how it relieves certain symptoms of multiple sclerosis,
- or how it corrects Crohn's disease,
- or how it reverses fibromyalgia
- or how it lowers high blood pressure yet elevates low blood pressure,
- or how it benefits virtually any ailment with autoimmune components.

Obviously, CMO is a general remedial immunomodulator that acts upon the memory T-cells which control the autoimmune processes within our bodies. Those who speculate otherwise have misunderstood the physiological actions of CMO within the body.

It is also important to understand that CMO acts *only* upon memory T-cells and does not inhibit the activities of any of the several other types of T-cells or protective immune system agents that are responsible for combating invading microorganisms or intrusive substances.

Unlike the immunosuppressants commonly used to try to temporarily control the symptoms of autoimmune diseases, CMO does not leave the body vulnerable to attack by disease-causing agents. Nor does it inhibit the body's resistance to tumor formation, as do the dangerous tumor necrosis factor (TNF) suppressants of some new arthritis drugs

Research summary

Some of the information that follows may be a bit complex for the average reader However, I am including these details because many people seek advice about CMO from their physicians. Altogether too often they've been told that them is nothing that could accomplish what CMO achieves, and that there is no "science" behind it. Well, though condensed and somewhat simplified, here's a brief look at some of the research that explains how CMO works. If it interests you, read it, if not, just skip it. CMO will do its job regardless. And don't hesitate to show this chapter to your doctor

Cetylmyristoleate, the original oily substance that eventually led to our research and development of CMO Cerasomal cis-9-cetylmyristoleate™ for oral administration, is a natural substance. It was not deliberately created, it was discovered in nature. Myristoleates are known to occur naturally in trace amounts in certain fatty tissues of only a few animals: cows, sheep, chickens, whales, beavers, and mice - although there may be a few others. For humans they occur in minute amounts as natural food components in butter, cheese, beef, chicken, lamb, and mutton. They also occur as natural food components for predatory animals that feed on any of the animals or foods mentioned. Their role in nutrition has not been studied, but they have never been known to cause harm. CMO is a safe, nontoxic, naturally derived substance. Certified laboratory toxicology testing proves it. These scientific tests certify CMO is nontoxic in massive doses and causes no harmful side effects. CMO achieved the safest rating class awarded.

Because it is a natural substance and not one designed and created with a specific purpose in mind, the precise pharmacodynamics of CMO are not clearly evident as they would be in the case of a substance that had been designed in the laboratory. Therefore, its biochemical and physiological effects must be determined by scientific investigation, analysis, and interpretation - not by a theory from which something has been specifically designed. Nevertheless, there is a strong foundation of scientific research concerning memory T-cells that gives us a basis of understanding regarding the mechanisms of action of CMO.

Cetylmyristoleate remained unnoticed for twenty years after its discovery until the research team of the San Diego International Immunological Center (SDC) unearthed it and developed it into a usable product ("CMO") early in 1995. There is no known research on cetylmyristoleate pharmacodynamics, and certainly none that has ever been published.

However it has long been established scientifically that myristoleate analogs are found in the composition of cell walls of living organisms. We believe that's what allows CMO to permeate the cell walls of memory T-cells to accomplish their mission. Our pharmacodynamic model of the immunomodulatory effects of CMO involves the naturally programmed functions of memory T-cells. Living cells of all kinds have a life-span or program that is predetermined by either time or function. Many cells are programmed to complete their life cycle according to a predetermined span of time. Others, like memory T-cells, are programmed to deactivate upon completing a specific function.

When the system errs it results in autoimmune or other problems that may result in ailments like arthritis, fibromyalgia, lupus, sarcoidosis, scleroderma, etc. - or the chronic inflammatory and autoimmune complications of other diseases like multiple sclerosis, emphysema, asthma, prostatitis, psoriasis, macular degeneration, tendinitis, sciatica, and others.

Remember, it's the memory T-cells that are responsible for perpetuating autoimmune disorders. They are the military "Generals" of the immune system that direct immune cell activities.

When a memory T-cells completes its function it is supposed to deactivate. We have learned that some memory T-cells avoid programmed deactivation. Virgin (naive, or unprogrammed) memory T-cells are stable, but following activation they can be maintained in continuous cycle by periodic re-stimulation from macrophages or other memory T-cells.

Normally, activated T-cells become increasingly unstable with each cycle of activation and rest, and are less likely to accept further re-stimulation. This process limits T-cell memory by preventing the continuous cycling of primed cells. This is a very important limiting mechanism that is vital to the prevention of excessive memory T-cell populations.

Nevertheless, some programmed cells revert to the stable state and are indistinguishable from naive cells. This is vital to avoid the complete loss of important defensive programs in a correctly functioning immune system. An extremely close correlation exists between the resting/naive memory T-cell populations and the programmed populations.

Studies also reveal that in arthritics, the synovial fluid in the joints is over-populated with programmed memory T-cells - and they are very resistant to deactivation. Studies performed with patients and in lab experiments indicate that this results from interaction with certain joint tissue (stromal cells in the pannus tissue). Gout does not involve proliferating pannus tissue.

This supports our clinical findings that CMO has less effect on gout than on rheumatoid, osteoarthritis, and other forms of arthritis.

Many diseases resolve themselves. Arthritis and most other autoimmune ailments do not. Studies show that the persistent inflammation that is characteristic of rheumatoid synovitis and other autoimmune ailments results from the persistence of memory T-cell populations.

Unlike memory T-cells, which don't engage in battle, other T-cells are directly combative. These sacrifice their lives to win. And at the end of an immune response the remaining excess cells are eliminated. It is a vital operation of the immune system. However, these cells still contain cytolytic molecules and are toxic. The spilling of some of these toxins may account for the mild Herxheimer (toxicity or "breakthrough pains") reaction that sometimes occurs with the use of CMO.

This new perception of memory T-cell function has yielded insights into disease processes such as viral infection, rheumatoid arthritis, lupus and many others. Lupus produces a broad spectrum of autoantibodies to cellular components. Studies show that patients with lupus actually have very high levels of expired cytotoxic cells that have not been effectively cleared. Inadequate clearance of these cells following infections is the likely source of the antigens that trigger the autoimmune process. This is true for virtually all disorders with autoimmune components and clearly explains the value of CMO for such diseases.

Yet in periods of health the number of T-cells present remains relatively constant. Contrary to conventional belief, resting memory T-cells also require continuous signals to stay active. These signals are found in blood and in even greater amounts at sites of inflammation such as the rheumatoid synovium. Resting memory T-cells are graded in the same way as activated cells: naive cells are stable, early primed cells are less so, and highly active cells are very unstable. The levels of signal required are much greater for activated cells.

Also, memory T-cells maintained at high density in culture do not need external signals for survival. They seem to signal each other. This activating mechanism appears to be similar to the stromal cell influence on memory T-cells, and in part explains the stability and survival of excessive memory T-cell populations.

Obviously much more research is necessary to understand all the complex mechanisms of memory T-cells and CMO in the control of autoimmune diseases. Studies are also being planned to better understand how CMO impacts on other diseases. Clinical evidence already clearly indicates that CMO affects virtually any ailment with chronic inflammatory or autoimmune components.

It also indicates that autoimmune processes can be triggered by many factors encountered in everyday life events. Another chapter of this book deals with how CMO can nip those processes in the bud and prevent them from developing into troublesome, and sometimes crippling, degenerative ailments.

Where can I find CMO?

There are only a few distributors that offer legitimate CMO, using the same form I tested in my medical clinics, and have demonstrated to be effective in with my patients. Unfortunately, there are also many ineffective products fraudulently labelled "CMO" being foisted on unsuspecting arthritis victims. The authenticity of the genuine product was confirmed in a recent court decision. A Federal District Court awarded monetary damages to the manufacturer of the genuine product as a result of a case filed against one impostor. We devote a whole chapter later in this book to help you identify and avoid those counterfeit products. Preying on the public by producing, would you believe, worthless counterfeit CMO! So look for products using certified CMO, such as CMO Cerasomal-cis-9-cetylmyristoleate™ fatty acids. In some parts of the world, including parts of Europe, the authentic product is individually certified with a coded serial number unique to each bottle of the authenticated product.

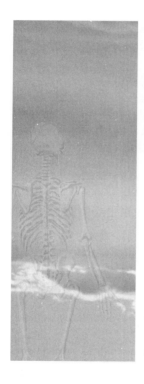

Chapter Two

CMO - Modern Miracle Against Arthritis?

CMO - Modern Miracle Against Arthritis?

The cure for arthritis - you'd think we were after the holy grail or something. It seemed so incredibly difficult and elusive. After all, medical science has been searching for it for centuries with nothing more to show than a few pain relievers and anti-inflammatory drugs. Nothing before even came close to being a cure.

Medical professionals are loathe to use the word miracle in the face of the most miraculous of circumstances. Nevertheless, the word keeps cropping up in physicians' reports about CMO. Dr. William C. Douglas titled his article *A New "Miracle Cure" for Arthritis* in the newsletter *Second Opinion*. Dr. Douglas Hunt used the word in his book *Boom You're Well*. And patients call it miraculous all the time. Even medical doctors who've sought relief from their own pain and suffering through various other remedies have used the expression liberally.

It's no wonder, for there have been virtually no truly significant advances in the treatment of arthritis since the times when people were chewing on willow tree bark to suck out its aspirin, or later the synthesis of aspirin by the German chemist Felix Hoffman in 1893. Medical science has made virtually no progress in the treatment of arthritis in over a hundred years. Pain killers and anti-inflammatory drugs are all we've had, and those just try to help relieve the symptoms. There's been absolutely nothing to treat the cause of arthritis. That is, not until now.

A revolutionary discovery - buried for 25 years

Back in the early 1970s a researcher in the employ of the U.S. Government National Institutes of Health (NIH) made a discovery. In a certain strain of laboratory rats he found a substance that not only made animals immune to getting arthritis, but also cured afflicted animals. The substance, originally extracted from ground up Swiss Albino Mice, is called cetylmyristoleate.

However, when the researcher reported his remarkable findings to his superiors in an attempt to secure funding for additional research, his request was mysteriously denied. Nevertheless, struggling along without authorization, he continued his studies and reported further successes. Strangely, not only were his requests for funding continuously denied, all of his accomplishments went completely unrecognized. Though they never said so directly, it was as though the NIH wanted him to abandon the project completely. Discouraged though he was, he still continued his research as best he could with absolutely no funding at all. When he retired about a decade later, since even the mere existence of his work went completely unacknowledged by the NIH, he took his discovery with him and continued the research on his own. And well he deserved to do so. Had he not, his discovery may never have come to light.

It has been reported that some time later, one by one he went to three different major pharmaceutical companies offering to share his discovery. One by one, his offers were rejected - not for lack of effectiveness, but because the product was derived from natural sources it could not be patented in a way to hog all the profits. The companies couldn't care less about the fact that it worked, only that they couldn't protect it from being manufactured by some competing company. Nor did they express any interest in funding further research on the project.

One could also speculate on the likelihood that by making available a product that potentially reverses the arthritic process permanently, it would kill their annual multi-billion dollar sales of existing arthritis products - all of which must be taken repeatedly for the rest of the arthritis victims' lives. Quite understandably, of course, the pharmaceutical companies love products that lead to a lifetime of repeat sales.

After its rejection by the pharmaceutical companies the project lay fallow for several years. No further attempts were made to explore its potential.

The chain of events that followed have never been made crystal clear. It has been reported that as some years passed, the researcher himself began to suffer terribly from arthritis and was receiving conventional medical therapy to treat it. It is important to note that despite the fact that he had explored the safety and effectiveness of his discovery on lower animals at the NIH, research had never reached the level of testing on higher animals. But once his arthritis reached excruciating extremes and his physician told him that he was beyond any effective help, the researcher decided to take a risk. He brewed up a batch of cetylmyristoleate at home and injected himself. Thus, he became the first person ever to receive the substance as a test of the discovery on human beings. We honour his courage.

It was a historic moment. He began to feel symptomatic relief the very next day, and soon he reached a point where he experienced total reversal of his arthritis. His doctor was astonished when he subsequently examined his patient and heard the whole story of the discovery.

The doctor was so impressed that he persuaded him to write an account of his research project. The doctor promised to help him get it published in the *Journal of Pharmaceutical Sciences*, hoping that the article might stimulate someone into continuing the exploration of the project. Then, early in 1995, a few months after the article appeared, that's exactly what happened. The San Diego Clinic International Immunological Centre (SDC) embarked on a project to develop the discovery into a usable product.

But long before that, it seems that several years had intervened between the self-injection and the actual publication of the article. Meanwhile, it has been reported, even though the substance was provided quite informally to a couple hundred more arthritis victims with astounding success, there was no formal progress in research or development.

The journal article itself didn't seem to stimulate much interest either. Perhaps that's because it was only three pages long and dealt solely with mouse model studies. Besides, it was reporting on research that took place over twenty years before. Perhaps the readers thought there couldn't be much value to something that had lain dormant so very long. Or maybe they thought there must have been more recent research that refuted the early findings. Nor did the article provoke questions about why it had been ignored by the NIH and how it came to buried for so long - except in one instance.

It's not easy turning a discovery into a miracle

When a research associate of the San Diego Clinic found the report, he immediately recognized its potential. Intense research on arthritis by that group had been ongoing for several years, spurred on in part by the personal interest of the clinic's director who himself was suffering from very severe osteoarthritis in both knees.

It wouldn't take long to produce a small quantity for some preliminary testing, but there were drawbacks. The original substance was effective as an injectable, but to make it readily available to the public, an oral form would have to be developed. As an orally administered product the original injectable form often produced diarrhea or upset the stomach. It was a heavy oil that resulted a gooey mess when put into capsules. Furthermore, not only was it difficult to digest, its bioavailability was very low. Low bioavailability results in very little of a product actually being assimilated in a form that's effective for its purpose in the body. That means more product is needed to accomplish its mission. And that drives up the cost, which was already very high as a result of the complexity in producing the substance.

Once the decision was made to try to develop an improved product, the original researcher was approached with an offer to join in the forthcoming project. For reasons not clearly expressed, he refused. Perhaps, as a result of the previous rejections, he felt there was no commercial value to the substance. Or he may have had other considerations. Whatever the reason, he rejected the offer.

What the new researchers were after would have to be quite different from the original, yet retain or improve on its effectiveness. Thanks to the genius of the biochemist who found the journal article, all of their goals were met. He was able to develop a product with high bioavailability when taken orally. Furthermore, it did not upset the stomach. Nor did it disturb the intestinal tract, except in the very most sensitive persons. And he managed to overcome one of the biggest hurdles: come up with a manufacturing process that was cost-effective. It was an amazing feat.

Finally, a product for the public

The result was cerasomal-cis-9-cetylmyristoleate, which bears the trademarked commercial name, CMO. Now CMO is quite different from the unmodified cetylmyristoleate which produces nausea, is so hard to digest, and has such a low level of bioavailability. In CMO, the cetylmyristoleate is phase stabilized using certain cerasomal technologies which makes it so much easier to assimilate through the intestine, disposes of the nausea problem, and gives it enormously higher levels of bioavailability. It also results in an end product that is a waxy solid rather than a messy oily liquid, making it much easier and neater to capsule. The end result was the commercially viable product available today: CMO. And that's the product so many people are calling a miracle because it has been so effective where all else has failed.

There are cases where people had been unable to walk up a flight of stairs for years, but they're doing it now - and painlessly, thanks to CMO. There are hundreds of cases where conventional treatments had reached a point where they were no longer of any benefit at all - yet CMO relieved all their symptoms. And many were very severe cases. Actually, there have been so many successes with extreme cases that they're not at all uncommon any more. Doctors keep reporting new ones every week. The specific details of many cases, some quite ordinary and some quite fascinating, will be reported in following chapters.

A warning about counterfeit CMO!

CMO has been so effective that there are even several counterfeit versions being produced by unscrupulous criminals preying upon unsuspecting arthritis victims and health product dealers. Their labels may even claim to be the original or authentic product, but they are not CMO. One of the following chapters describes most of these counterfeit products and explains how to verify your product source.

A Federal Court in California has sent a clear message that it recognizes the authenticity of CMO and will not tolerate the infringement of counterfeiters upon the authentic product.

The United States District Court in Orange, California recently awarded a half million dollars in damages in a judgment against Advanced Labs of Redding, California as a result of a suit filed against them alleging trademark infringement, false advertising, and unfair competition, claiming that those practices resulted in consumer confusion and loss of sales of authentic CMO products.

The CMO mark has been used since November 1995 to clearly and specifically identify the proprietary cerasomal-cis-9-cetylmyristoleate product. CMO is a natural immunomodulator used by people suffering from such ailments as arthritis, Crohn's disease, carpal tunnel syndrome, fibromyalgia, emphysema, migraine headaches, prostate inflammation, and several other ailments with autoimmune involvement.

Still, those phony products keep cropping up. Remember, it's buyer beware. If you have any doubts about some product, you're welcome to call the San Diego Clinic for confirmation of its authenticity. See Chapter Nine for details and contact information, and Chapter Eight for more on counterfeit products.

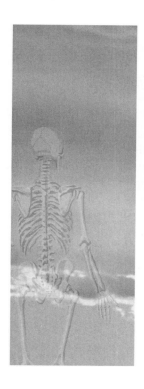

Chapter Three

What Makes CMO so Different from all the Other Remedies You've Tried?

What Makes CMO so Different from all the Other Remedies You've Ever Tried?

What makes CMO so different? Well, the most important difference is that it works!

We know that sounds arrogant, but it's true. CMO does stop the arthritic process at its source. It doesn't treat the symptoms of arthritis, it treats the cause at its point of origin: the immune system. The same holds true not just for arthritis, but for many other ailments with autoimmune components as well.

Again let us refer to the *TIME* magazine article of October 28, 1996. It says, "The [arthritis] problem starts when, for reasons no one fully understands, a few misguided T-cells incite other immune-system cells called macrophages to attack the joints." That's why arthritis is referred to as an "autoimmune" disease - because your body is attacked by your own immune cells. It's like having a bad computer program in your immune system.

As explained in Chapter 1, it's those "misguided T-cells" in the immune system which are directing the attacks against the cartilage in the joints of the body and are causing the symptoms of arthritis pain and inflammation. Those "misguided T-cells" are more properly known as memory T-cells, which in this case have been erroneously programmed to attack healthy cartilage as well as unhealthy and damaged cartilage.

Treating the cause of arthritis, not just the symptoms

For the past hundred years the only weapons medical practitioners and pharmacists have had in their arsenal were directed against those symptoms of pain and inflammation. But now there's CMO, a naturally derived product that targets the root cause of arthritis rather than trying to just relieve the symptoms.

First of all, let's emphasize the fact that CMO is not a conventional product. It is not a cortisone or other steroid. It is not some kind of pain reliever. CMO is a natural immunomodulator. There's never been anything like it before for the treatment of arthritis (or hardly anything else for that matter). It was discovered by a researcher employed at the U.S. Government National Institutes of Health (NIH) more than 25 years ago, and only recently brought to light. Its has the unique ability to act against the cause of arthritis - normalizing the response of your own immune system. Its abilities are so profound it may well revolutionize the way all autoimmune ailments will be treated in the future.

What's an immunomodulator?

Just what is meant by the word immunomodulator? The action of any "modulator" is to bring a function or condition from some state of irregularity to a state of normalcy. Its job is put things that were out of whack back to normal again.

CMO is a natural immunomodulator that literally acts to modulate the immune response and bring it back to normal. That's far beyond the scope of any common arthritis medication. The affliction of arthritis is not a normal state of the body. It is not normal for the body to try to destroy healthy parts of itself. CMO acts to return the body to its normal state. It acts to normalize the immune system and stop those destructive attacks.

As a natural immunomodulator, it serves to naturally regulate a function, which in the case of arthritis, has been mistakenly programmed to direct certain immune cells to destroy healthy cartilage along with the cartilage that has been damaged by trauma or some invading organism. It's very much like having a bad computer program. But once you fix the program, you fix the problem. And once it's fixed, it stays fixed. Normally there's no need for any further medication. People who were successfully treated nine or ten years ago have been free of the need for arthritis medication ever since.

That's because CMO does not try to directly treat the symptoms of arthritis pain and inflammation. Instead, by getting at the cause of the problem, it stops the arthritic process itself. Once the errant immune system has been normalized the destruction stops, and the pain and inflammation are automatically relieved by your own body's healing mechanisms.

In conventional treatment, attempts are made to control the pain and inflammation of arthritis through the use of ordinary medications. But even when the symptoms are controlled successfully, the attacks against your cartilage continue because those medications treat only the symptoms, not the cause. Eventually those medications begin to lose their effect. It's not just because your body has built up tolerance, but also because the arthritic process has not been checked and it continues to worsen. Even drastically increasing the dosage of ordinary medications often doesn't help much after a number of years.

Furthermore, relieving the pain in afflicted joints without improving their condition may actually be harmful. It can encourage the progressive destruction of those joints, which, in many cases, ought not to be overstressed. Any damaged joint is even more easily and more severely damage if it is abused. Masking the pain in such joints facilitates the possibility of such abuse. The case history related in Chapter 5 is a prime example of codeine abuse.

When the arthritic process itself remains unchecked, gradually more and more misprogrammed memory T-cells are generated, producing increasingly voluminous macrophage attacks against joint cartilage. As healthy cartilage is destroyed, your body tries to replace it by generating new cartilage. Unfortunately, the attacks eventually reach the point where they exceed your body's ability to replace the amount destroyed. That's when joint deterioration soon becomes a very serious and painful problem. Your body reaches a point where it quickly loses ground against the disease. Time and time again we've heard people say that for years their arthritis was just a bit of a bother - then suddenly it worsened.

Often, arthritis can progress from an annoyance into a serious crippling problem in just a few months. Obviously, it's best to correct the problems of arthritis before any permanent damage has been inflicted.

How quickly does CMO take effect?

With the intervention of CMO, the arthritic process is halted and the body can then heal itself quite naturally. The pain and inflammation usually disappear promptly as a result of the body's own natural healing abilities. When CMO stops the arthritic process, the body heals itself. The speed with which that happens varies a great deal from one person to another. The state of one's overall health, apart from the severity of the arthritis itself, affects one's healing process. Individual healing ability is one of the major determining factors influencing the rapidity of the recovery.

Most people begin to improve in about four to seven days. Many respond overnight. The benefits may appear quite gradually, or they may be felt all at once. A few people failed to see any benefit at all for four to six weeks after finishing all their capsules. For them, it was an eternity of disappointment. Then when their symptoms disappeared, it came as quite a surprise because at first it seemed that the treatment had failed completely. Apparently the CMO had halted the arthritic process, but the body was slow to heal so the benefits were slow to appear. That's certainly rare, but it's happened several times over the years.

On the other hand, there are overnight successes. With the first formal introduction of CMO at the national medical conference on ageing at Las Vegas in December 1995, all five of the doctors who tried CMO for their own arthritis responded quickly. Three of them responded overnight, while one took two days and the other took three days to experience the complete reversal of their symptoms. There's just no telling how quickly or how long it may take for someone to fully enjoy the benefits of their own healing processes.

How often does CMO succeed?

Over eighty-five percent of the thousands of people who've taken CMO have had a 70% to 100% improvement in joint mobility with corresponding reduction of pain and inflammation.

No ordinary medication gets results like that. Yet CMO, this natural healer derived from the fatty tissue of beef, produces astonishing results for nearly everyone who tries it. Its results, both in the medical trials described in a following chapter and its use by physicians and other health practitioners in day-to-day applications, have been consistently stable.

That is certainly much more than can be said for the conventional pain relievers and anti-inflammatory medications. Many arthritis victims reach a point where common medications are of no help at all. In the *TIME* article, a doctor speaks of having gone "15 years without anything new to treat my patients."

The effects of CMO may last forever

Because it acts against the cause of arthritis, the benefits seem to last indefinitely. Normally it takes only one full set of capsules to "reset" the immune system. Once that happens you are usually free of the need to take any further arthritis medication ever again - including CMO !

Imagine the possibility of being freed forever of the need to take any more arthritis medication. That's what usually happens with a successful CMO treatment. You're freed of the relentless and aggravating need to be constantly popping pills. It even frees you of the CMO itself!

Side effects

Unlike all the usual pain killers and anti-inflammatory medications, CMO is a naturally derived substance. It is nature's own immunomodulator, derived from fatty bovine (beef) tissue. As such it has no more direct side effects than that of eating a pat of butter. A later chapter deals with the safety of CMO and the toxicity of many frequently used prescription and nonprescription drugs. (Did you know, for example, that even prolonged use of the presumably innocuous medication Tylenol can damage your liver?).

So many simple non-prescription pain relievers and anti-inflammatory drugs can have serious side effects. Yet, doctors get pushed by their desperate patients into prescribing such truly horrible drugs as Methotrexate. The *Physicians' Desk Reference* of pharmaceutical drugs (your doctor's oversized "drug bible") contains 4½ columns of fine-print precautions, adverse reactions, warnings, and contraindications. It states,

"There is a potential for severe toxic reactions." That statement comes from the manufacturer of Methotrexate itself. It is one of the most toxic drugs ever made. And doctors know it. Yet when suffering patients plead for their doctors to "please, please do something for me," the temptation to prescribe damaging drugs like Methotrexate or cortisones becomes altogether too strong.

But there's no need for such drastic measures any longer. CMO halts the arthritic process without any harmful side effects. Thousands have done it already. Probably you can, too. The odds are about nine to one in your favour.

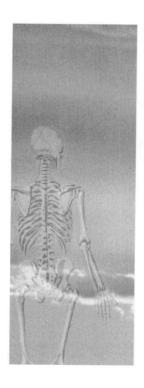

Chapter Four

Answering Your Most Frequently Asked Questions

Answering Your Most Frequently Asked Questions

This chapter will try to briefly answer just about all the questions that have ever been asked about CMO with respect to what it is, what it does, how it works, etc. Look for more complete explanations in other chapters.

The absolutely unchallenged number one most frequently asked question about CMO is:

What makes CMO so different from all the dozens of other remedies I've ever tried?

All of Chapter 3 of this book was devoted to answering that particular question. However, to make this chapter complete and independent, a brief summary is presented right here.

Unlike anything else in existence for the treatment of arthritis, CMO is a natural immunomodulator. It is not a pain reliever. It is not an anti-inflammatory medication. It is not a cortisone or other steroid. Its effects on arthritis are totally unique. Instead of treating the symptoms of pain and inflammation, CMO capsules act directly against the cause of arthritis. It acts to normalize an immune system that has gone astray. It modulates the attacks against the cartilage in your joints. Once the immune problem is regulated, the attacks on your joints will stop and the symptoms of pain and inflammation will be corrected by your own body's natural healing process. Usually one set of capsules is all that's needed to 'reset' the immune system and halt the arthritic process. Normally, once the attacks are stopped and your body heals itself, no further medications of any kind are ever needed.

Does that mean a person needs to take CMO only once and that's it?

Many arthritis victims need to take only one full set of CMO capsules over a period of a couple of weeks to be free of arthritis pain and inflammation, probably forever. No further medication is necessary, not even CMO. You do not have to continue taking the CMO. Once it has succeeded in doing its job, you are set free of that need to be constantly taking any kind of arthritis pills, be it once or several times a day.

Does it work for both rheumatoid and osteoarthritis?

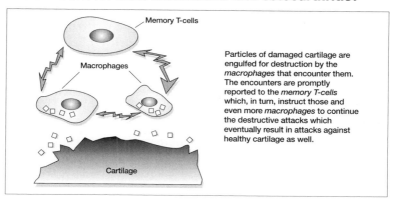

Memory T-cells

Macrophages

Cartilage

Particles of damaged cartilage are engulfed for destruction by the *macrophages* that encounter them. The encounters are promptly reported to the *memory T-cells* which, in turn, instruct those and even more *macrophages* to continue the destructive attacks which eventually result in attacks against healthy cartilage as well.

Despite the conventional view that osteoarthritis is not an autoimmune disease, it seems quite clear that autoimmune processes are nevertheless involved in the continuing attacks against joint cartilage, just as they are in rheumatoid arthritis attacks. This is clearly contradictory to all existing medical theories, and we suspect that this may generate considerable controversy in the medical community. Nevertheless, it is quite evident to us that osteoarthritis, as well as rheumatoid arthritis, is an autoimmune disease.

The particles of damaged cartilage resulting from the traumas that initiate osteoarthritis are gobbled up by macrophages in the same way as the particles of cartilage resulting from rheumatoid arthritis. Regardless of whether they are produced as a result of some organism initiating rheumatoid arthritis or whether they are produced as the result of some physical trauma initiating osteoarthritis, the damaged cartilage particles trigger the same response from the macrophages that results in the faulty programming of the immune system's memory T-cells.

Since CMO acts to halt the macrophage attacks against the cartilage, it has proved to be effective against both rheumatoid and osteoarthritis. That's further evidence that osteoarthritis is an autoimmune disease. CMO has often proved beneficial for several other types of arthritis as well. A few of those other types include those associated with Reiter's syndrome, ankylosing spondylitis, Sjögren's syndrome, psoriatic arthritis, and Behçet's syndrome. It has also been found to relieve various types of back pain of undetermined origin (probably arthritis related or having autoimmune components involving chronic inflammation).

Will CMO improve joint mobility?

As long as the joint can be moved however slightly (either by the afflicted person or even by someone else), joint mobility can usually be restored in full or at least in part. The vast majority of users benefit by a 100% improvement. Most others improve by at least 70%. Even a 70% improvement is highly significant to persons whose joint mobility is severely limited.

Impairment of joint mobility is usually the result of inflammation and/or pain impeding the movement. Once CMO does away with the inflammation, the pressure on the joint is gone and so is the interference with the movement. The pain is also relieved when the inflammation subsides.

However, if the bones in the joint have been damaged or have fused together, only surgery is likely to help those particular joints. CMO can halt the arthritic process, but it cannot repair physical damage to bone itself.

Does CMO stop arthritis pain?

Arthritis pain will be reduced by nearly 100% in almost every instance. A small percentage of people experienced reductions of only 70% to 90%, which was still of such great benefit that it allowed them to function quite normally again. Apart from the clinical study, in practical use about 10% to 15% showed only 0% to 50% improvement.

Does CMO reduce inflammation?

Yes, and it does so quite effectively. The pressure of the inflammation in the joints is the major cause of arthritis pain, stiffness, and deformation. Inflammation will be reduced by nearly 100% in almost every instance. A small percentage of people experienced reductions of only 70% to 90%. Additional improvements of 10% to 20% were often seen with the use of a second set of capsules.

How long before CMO takes effect?

Most people begin to feel relief within two to four days. Sometimes that's all it takes. Others may take a bit longer, and, rarely, some may even need a few weeks. There have been a few very rare cases where little or no benefit was experienced until up to six weeks after finishing a complete set of capsules.

Can it correct deformities?

More often than not, it does. Deformed fingers and toes are frequently the result of the inflammation which swells the joints and pushes the bones out of place. Reduction of the swelling alone improves appearance dramatically and often allows the dislocated bones to return to their normal positions. However, extreme cases may require some physical therapy.

What about really severe cases?

Although there can never be any absolute guarantee of success, even most persons previously confined to bed or otherwise drastically limited have responded dramatically. Many are no longer dependent on others for care. A number of these severe cases received additional benefit from repeating the treatment one more time. Several others found that physical therapy or controlled exercise programs were also helpful.

What about joints where the cartilage is completely worn away?

Unless the bones have fused together, the usual problem is not lack of mobility, but pain. The majority of such drastic cases have responded favourably, resulting in painless movement, even in the knees. More research is needed to track the regeneration of cartilage in severely eroded joints.

Does it work for everyone?

For CMO to be able to work its immunomagic, it often depends upon good liver function and a good digestive system. If your digestive system cannot assimilate the CMO, then it just passes through the gut without ever being absorbed. Digestive incapacity is usually caused by the presence of large numbers of intestinal parasites, the accumulation of impacted waste matter, frequent diarrhea, or a deficiency of certain digestive enzymes. These problems must usually be corrected before one can get the full benefit of CMO. Once the CMO is assimilated, proper liver function is critical to success. Liver function impairment can result from diseases like hepatitis, mononucleosis (EBV), or others. It also results from alcohol or steroid abuse. Overuse of some very common medications like Tylenol can also be the cause of liver damage. People with liver or digestive problems may need special attention prior to and during the CMO program to improve their chances of success.

Can I continue my usual medications while taking CMO?

Yes, except for Methotrexate (also known as Rheumatrex). This dangerously toxic anti-cancer drug is sometimes prescribed for arthritis as well. It is one of the leading causes of pharmaceutical liver damage and impairment. Sometimes to the point of death. And it completely destroys the beneficial effects of CMO. If you cannot manage without it, you can still try CMO, but success is less likely. Nevertheless, we have seen several dramatic recoveries in persons taking Methotrexate. Surprisingly, CMO ended up solving their problems with liver inflammation as well reversing their arthritis.

As for other medications, a few days after starting CMO, you probably won't need them any more. As your condition improves, try cutting down on the amounts of your usual medications. However, it's best to avoid or reduce the use of steroids as much as possible and as soon as possible before or during the CMO therapy. The sooner they're reduced or eliminated, the sooner you're likely to get the maximum benefit from your CMO.

Always check with your physician before reducing or discontinuing any prescribed medications.

Is there a special diet involved?

There are certain foods that will interfere in the action of CMO so they must be eliminated or limited to an absolute minimum for about four weeks only. Alcohol, chocolate, black tea, coffee and other caffeinated drinks must be avoided completely. Potatoes, tomatoes, eggplant, and peppers may need to be limited. The consumption of fats, oils, legumes, and grains must be reduced. Meats, fish, poultry and eggs may be eaten without any limitation. Most vegetables and fruits are unrestricted as well. At the end of the four week program, you may resume your normal eating routine.

Is there an exercise program required?

No special exercises are necessary. The absence of pain and return of joint mobility is so profound that normal activities will follow quite naturally. Unfortunately, the usual tendency is to overindulge in the new-found freedom. This frequently results in a bit of soreness in muscles that had gone so long unused.

Is it okay to exercise?

Yes. Many people want to shed the extra pounds put on by the lack of activity resulting from the limitations forced upon them by the arthritis. Many others want to rebuild muscle strength once they are free to do so again painlessly. But, as with all sound fitness programs, it's best to do so gradually, building strength or losing weight without trauma. Your body will need time to readjust, so just take it easy for a while. If you decide you want a fitness trainer, be sure to explain your condition. With the pain of arthritis relieved, many individuals tend to overdo their activities and exercises.

Is CMO expensive?

The cost of treatment is very modest. Most arthritis victims are already spending more on anti-inflammation and pain medications in just a few months. CMO is a real bargain compared to things like gold shots and many other treatments. Since you usually need to take only one set of capsules, it actually saves thousands of dollars in the long run. And it's great to be free of the constant pill-popping syndrome as well.

Is age a factor?

Not really. That's a question usually asked by elderly individuals. Actually, people of all ages have responded perfectly, even many well over 80 years old. Although arthritis becomes far more common with advancing age, even very young children are sometimes afflicted. Children as young as eight years of age suffering from juvenile onset arthritis have responded perfectly.

What causes arthritis?

It seems to be initiated by the immune system's desire to eliminate particles of damaged or unhealthy cartilage from the body. Those cartilage particles may result from physical damage or from invading organisms that have attacked the joints. Diseases like rheumatic fever and maybe even the flu virus are often responsible. (Remember those aching joints that sometimes come with a flu attack?).

As explained earlier in Chapter 1 and in the question about rheumatoid and osteoarthritis, an immune response develops and macrophage cells are then directed to attack those fragments of damaged or unhealthy cartilage. But the macrophages that are instructed to gobble up the cartilage don't distinguish between unhealthy and healthy cartilage and eventually a major onslaught against the healthy cartilage in the joints begins as well.

Unfortunately, there's no 'stop button' or 'end program' command in the immune system and the attacks continue even after all the unhealthy or damaged cartilage has been destroyed. They often become more severe with time because more and more of the memory T-cells that direct the macrophage attacks are generated. Thus, left unchecked, arthritis usually continues to worsen with the passage of time. Severe rheumatoid arthritis is believed to sometimes shorten the life span by as much as twenty years.

How does CMO work?

CMO corrects the root cause of arthritis by normalizing the immune response and halting the destructive arthritic process. Then your body can begin to heal and repair itself without the interference of continuing attacks. Joints soon begin to heal. The pain and inflammation disappear. Although the major benefits usually come promptly, minor improvements may continue for several months after finishing your CMO. Improvement through the regeneration of cartilage may continue for years. With the pain and inflammation relieved, the joints often can function again quite normally despite minor physical damage that may have affected the bones of certain joints.

How do you know CMO has this normalizing action?

It is evident by CMO's effects on other autoimmune functions and diseases. Blood pressure is a good example. Whether it's high or low, when individuals take CMO, the blood pressure tends to normalize. That is, people with high blood pressure find that it drops; and people with low blood pressure find that it elevates. Even individuals suffering from lupus have seen their sedimentation rates normalize. There's nothing else in the world that has been able to do that for lupus victims.

Is it harmful in any way?

Studies relating to CMO began some 25 years ago at the U.S. Government National Institutes of Health (NIH). More recently, in 1995, clinical applications studies were conducted by the San Diego Clinic Immunological Centre in Chula Vista, California. No short or long-term negative side effects were ever observed in humans or in laboratory animals even at extremely high doses. Substances very closely related to CMO have been used in many common foods including hundreds of varieties of cheeses and chocolates as well as pharmaceutical pill coatings and cosmetic products. The safety of this naturally derived product has also been confirmed by independent laboratory toxicity studies.

What is CMO? Where does it come from?

Cerasomal-cis-9-cetylmyristoleate is the scientific biochemical name. CMO is the trademarked commercial name. It is a perfectly natural substance found in several common animals such as cows, sheep, chickens, beavers, mice, and whales. As supplied in capsules, CMO is a highly purified and refined waxy ester prepared for oral administration. It is wholly derived from certain natural fatty bovine (beef) tissue from American cows.

Is there any other way to find permanent relief?

Yes. According to the *Journal of Rheumatology (1993; 20: 137-140)* bone marrow transplants seem to have succeeded in reversing the arthritic process in two very remarkable cases.

Do you guarantee cure?

No responsible medical authority would ever guarantee a cure for any ailment. The world has yet to discover any treatment or medication, no matter how successful, that works for every one every time. However, in case of difficulties, the staff of the San Diego Clinic is happy to consult with you and your doctor to try to investigate and resolve any problems.

Does CMO work on pets and other animals?

Animals somehow seem to have responded even more favourably than humans. We have never seen a single failure with an animal! That may be because they are less likely to have been pharmaceutically abused with harmful medications. And certainly they don't have the peculiar psychological resistance we sometimes encounter in some humans.

The size of the animal does not seem to matter. CMO has been successful in treating dogs, cats, hamsters, pot-bellied pigs, horses, goats, and other animals. Dosages are adjusted to the size of the animal's immune system, not its weight. Horses, for example, that weigh ten times more than humans usually require only three or four bottles of CMO, not ten. Cats, on the other hand, need only about twenty capsules to be able to annoy you by jumping up on your kitchen counter again.

It may take a bit of imagination to dose certain animals for whom it's impossible to administer whole capsules. Most animals don't care for the taste of CMO, so it must be mixed into some favourite, highly flavoured food to mask the taste.

To our knowledge, CMO has never yet been administered to a bird, a reptile, an amphibian, or a fish, but we'd love to see the results.

Is CMO used for any other ailments?

There are several physicians whose investigations include CMO as a part of their therapeutic protocol (often along with their usual medications) for other disorders that seem to have certain autoimmune components. In most cases CMO appears to have played a very significant role in assisting recovery from those ailments.

These disorders, many of which are discussed in chapter 11, include migraine and cluster headaches, carpal tunnel syndrome, emphysema, lupus erythematosus, fibromyalgia, scleroderma, benign prostate hyperplasia, TMJ (painful jaw syndrome), ankylosing spondylitis, silicone breast disease, myasthenia gravis, Crohn's disease, multiple sclerosis, simple asthma, and back and foot pains of undetermined origins. The number of cases have been very limited, and significantly more elaborate and intensive investigations are needed before any conclusions can even begin to be drawn. Nevertheless, many very dramatic reversals and improvements in those afflictions have been noted by numerous responsible physicians.

We recently had a meeting with some European physicians who flew all the way to San Diego just to discuss CMO. They have been astounded by its success in helping treat several very stubborn diseases in which they are even more keenly interested.

As Dr. Douglas Hunt (MD) has stated, "CMO may well revolutionize the way all autoimmune diseases may be treated in the future."

No treatment of any kind should ever be undertaken without the professional supervision of a physician or other competent health care professional.

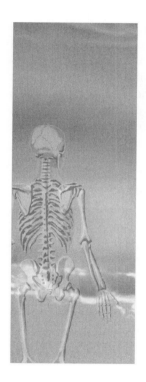

Chapter Five

A Very Personal History

A Very Personal History

A month or so after one subject found relief from the terrible pain and limitations of his arthritis he wrote a brief testimonial about his experience with CMO. Excerpts from that testimonial have appeared from time to time in our CMO information packages. Now that he has been free of virtually all pain for three years, he has also consented to prepare this more detailed "before and after" account for this book. Here's the story of his own experiences with arthritis and how his motives, both personal and professional, propelled the San Diego Clinic's research associates to the discovery and development of CMO. This is the compelling personal account of the Director of the San Diego Clinic.

"Two years ago I was a closet cripple; bone-on-bone in my knees. Then CMO turned my life around."

Following several years of excruciating pain from bone grinding against bone in my knees, I find it hard to believe that I'm still 95% pain free almost three years after taking CMO. It's a miracle! Up until then, I was what you might call a closet cripple, hiding the severity of my osteoarthritis from just about everyone but the chief of our research staff. I never was a complainer. I hid my pain. I pretended, as much as possible, that I wasn't suffering every minute of my waking day. The only time I was reasonably comfortable was when I was planted in my bed or on the sofa watching TV. Even then I couldn't cross my legs. In fact, there were only a couple of positions I could manage where my knees wouldn't hurt, and then only if I shifted my legs around frequently enough.

But that's just the tip of the iceberg. I'm going to tell you more, much more. I want you to understand why I had such a personal interest in constantly prodding our research associates into pursuing every conceivable avenue of investigation regarding arthritis. I'm sure they thought of me as some kind of possessed maniac. Remember, I was trying to hide my pain from nearly everyone. But how successfully can you hide it when you have to walk down a flight of stairs backwards?

Whenever I assisted our MDs in our patient examination and treatment rooms, I'd just scoot around like some wind-up toy on one of those wheeled stools that doctors always use. That way no one had to see my tortured walk. But I couldn't get up without pushing myself up from the seat with my arms. (The same was true for any chair or seat.) Sometimes I'd just get stuck there on that stool for quite a while. But most of the time I'd have a table or a desk to use for additional support to push myself up. Even so, getting up from anywhere meant I'd get those stabbing pains in my knees. Once I was seated somewhere, I tended to stay put for a long time. A very long time. I was sure my butt was beginning to mould itself into a chairseat shape.

Regardless, there I was, relentless about continuing research. Whip in hand, I was ruthless about all their snivelling complaints that they had already exhausted all avenues of exploration. Mush, you huskies! For me, pain was a great motivator and constant pain was an even greater one. So I couldn't have cared less about their calling me Dr. Strangelove. Or Robo-doc.

Most people probably thought it weird that I'd move a chair over to some object that I needed to pick up off the floor. I couldn't bend down, of course. So I'd sit on the chair and lean down sideways to pick things up. Maybe I wasn't so good at hiding my problem after all.

My evenings weren't much better. I couldn't cross my legs in bed either. If I chose to lie on my back, I'd have to prop a pillow under my knees. When I slept, it was always on my side with a baby pillow in between my knees. I couldn't stand the weight of one knee upon the other. Even with the cushion, several times a night I'd be shocked into wakefulness by some jolt of pain. I often wondered what our neighbours thought about those late night screams.

Naturally, as a medical professional, I was aware of mostly everything in the world used to treat arthritis. And, believe me, if I heard of it I tried it. (Except for steroids and Methotrexate. I wasn't willing to sacrifice my immune system and my liver.) It didn't matter if it was herbal, or homeopathic, or acupuncture, or gold shots, or conventional medicine, or voodoo, I tried it.

Yes, even voodoo. After several years of constant pain I even tried a couple of faith healers and a few very reputable Mexican 'curanderos' as well. I was assaulted by healing hands, dusted with magical powders, rubbed with potent poultices, thrashed with leafy branches, suffocated with smoky fumes, and stung by angry bees. I wasn't about to rule anything out. But it didn't help a bit.

I have a lot of respect for Oriental and Indian medicines. So I was hopeful when, in 1994, our researchers came up with some strange Ayurvedic medicine from India that was really supposed to work. There were many anecdotal reports of success, centuries of them. Lots of professional documentation as well. I spent months faithfully smearing my knees every night with some smelly Ayurvedic gooey tar and wrapping them in flannel and plastic to try to keep the goo from oozing out onto the bed. It oozed out anyway, just like some kind of killer alien blob of tar-like sulphured molasses, staining our sheets. What a mess! And no success.

I was also taking the whole range of vitamins and minerals, plus alfalfa, yucca, saw palmetto, juice diets, raw food diets, fasting, gelatin, shark cartilage, chicken cartilage, glucosamines, chondroitin sulfate, all kinds of herbs alone and in combination. Some were a help, but they could only dull the symptoms a bit, and certainly could not keep up with the rampant destruction of the cartilage in my knees. I must say, though, that I felt considerably more discomfort any day that I didn't take my supplements. So I kept on with them for the minimal benefits they brought, despite the fact that they were costing me a bundle.

Anti-inflammatory pills? Knowing how hard they are on the liver, I only took what I needed to keep on functioning. I could usually get away with only one or two strong (and very expensive) time-release pills on a working day. I'd gulp one down just before brushing my teeth in the morning. You see, for the most part I could run the clinic sitting behind my desk. I hardly had to move around at all, so that let me get through the day fairly well. But often I'd need another potent pill around mid-afternoon.

When the family would go to the movies or anywhere else that required some walking, I'd have to take a double dose (despite the medical warnings not to). Even so, trying to negotiate a set of any more than two stairs was a killer. So was the inclined aisle you have to descend to get to your movie seats. Going downhill was much worse than coming back up. And going down any flight of stairs was worse than climbing up. If you've got arthritis in your knees, I'm sure you know what I mean. I never shopped at the malls. Too much walking. Just a few yards of walking and I was in severe pain. I'd pick stores where I could park near the door. And ones with shopping carts were a must. They were very helpful to lean on while walking or scanning the merchandise. I found that wheelchair ramps were easier to negotiate than stairs.

Handrails were a blessing for pulling myself up and bracing myself to go down the ramps or stairs. I'm sure I looked like some funny stiff-legged mechanical teddy bear trying to negotiate sets of even just a few stairs.

Picking things up off the floor near a table or a desk wasn't so bad. Painful, yes. But at least I could do it by supporting myself with one hand while carefully bending down to pick up the object with the other hand - all the while hoping my knees wouldn't collapse. You know, you learn to cope.

Nevertheless, in my heart I knew that someday I'd reach the point where I'd be facing a dreaded wheelchair existence. I was already often using a cane and sometimes crutches. Next would come the crutches full time. Then the walker. And finally the wheelchair. I hated the thought of being so limited. Until I got arthritis I was always quite active - tennis, swimming, scuba diving, hiking, travelling, window shopping, or just strolling around here and there. It depressed me to have given up those pleasures.

It depressed me even more to think of how much of a burden I would become to my family.

In the beginning

The arthritic process had begun years ago, of course. It doesn't happen overnight. Though the terrible worsening seemed to have come suddenly, it had been building up for quite some time.

It all started with a vehicle accident that resulted in a terrible jolt to my knees. (I'll confess. It was a 55 mph dump off a motorcycle.) No broken bones, but my body was wracked with pain - especially my legs and back. I was in bed for two days, on crutches for two weeks, and using a cane for two months. Then it all went away, or so I thought, for about three years. I was just fine for three years. No sign of any trouble at all. But of course, the arthritic process had already begun with the big jolt. I didn't realize it then but, unnoticed, it was slowly building up steam, and it would soon blow up.

Then, I felt the first signs of what was really happening inside my body. A twinge of pain here, a bit of weakness there. Nothing dramatic. Hardly noticeable. Just a little hint of the misery to come.

Over the next three or four years the worsening was gradual. The pain, though mild, became almost ever-present during my waking hours. Soon I developed a click in my right knee that would sometimes give me quite a shot of pain when it snapped.

Then came the era of codeine abuse

I knew it was wrong, but I didn't know what else to do. We had been planning this leisurely round-the-world trip for years to celebrate a wedding anniversary. I wasn't about to let my arthritis spoil it.

Several years had passed since my accident and we were living in Spain at the time. The click in my knee had degenerated into a 'trick knee' that would sometimes buckle quite unexpectedly. Anti-inflammation and pain medication, including codeine, were readily available over the counter without prescription there. I used them only on particularly bad or particularly active days. But good days were coming far less frequently.

Then it was time for our trip, the dream vacation of a lifetime - a full year of bumming around Asia, the Pacific islands, and the Middle East. No schedule. Our bargain round-the-world tickets would let us linger anywhere as long as we liked. We could make our continuing flight reservations whenever we chose. Now how was I going to let my arthritis spoil a trip like that?

I knew there would be plenty of walking for museums, tours, sightseeing, and shopping. Then there'd be the scuba diving, swimming, boating, and beach bumming. A lot of activity - just the way we loved it. All joyfully accompanied by our vigorous eight-year-old son.

There was only one way I was going to make it through a year of that kind of activity: codeine. I gave no thought to the consequences of the abuse my already degenerating knees would suffer. Moreover, I wasn't about to rob a moment of the joy and adventure of this trip from anyone, myself included. I'm not for a moment going to pretend that I wasn't doing it for myself as well.

I didn't have to stockpile a whole year's supply of codeine. I knew it would be readily available in most of the countries we planned to visit. And it was. I'd go in and buy out the entire stock of two or three pharmacies at a time. It wasn't that much; they only stocked a half dozen boxes each. (Or so they said.) Except for India; there codeine was really cheap and I could get a couple hundred tablets at just one pharmacy. I really stocked up in India.

No I didn't turn into a junkie. Never got addicted. On boat cruises or lazy beach days, for example, I didn't bother taking codeine at all. And I didn't need it for swimming or diving either.

On museum, sightseeing, or shopping days, though, I'd really toss them down. And there were a lot of those days. But they were very low dose pills. I'd take several at a time - just about every four hours. Nobody noticed. Everyone's used to my vitamin regimen - gulping down nearly twenty pills with every meal. It was just routine.

My non-codeine days let me know, though, what I was doing to my knees. The tension, the stiffness, and the discomfort made it clear. Masking the pain let me remain active, but vigorous activity is not recommended for arthritic joints. It only hastens the degeneration of the already damaged and far more vulnerable cartilage. And we prolonged it by extending our vacation far beyond our originally scheduled year. It was the best of times for us, and the worst of times for my knees.

The mills of arthritis grind slowly ...

Returning home, I assessed the damages. Now I could relax and let my knees go without medication to try to evaluate their condition. The extended time of strenuous use during vacation had taken its toll. Stairs were more difficult to climb, and getting up from a low sofa was almost impossible.

I had no regrets about the trip. Even without the abuse, my arthritis would have continued to worsen, and I speculated that it had been my last chance ever to enjoy an experience like that anyway.

I knew where my ailment would take me. I was, eventually, destined to end up in a wheelchair. Or at the very least I'd need knee replacement surgery, which was not generally very successful in those days. Despite my long experience as the owner and director of a hospital as well as several clinics, I've never been fond of surgery.

... but they grind exceeding small

After the vacation I was careful to treat my knees gently, and despite the severe effects of that experience, further deterioration did not occur at an abnormally fast rate. It was constantly evident, slowly grinding away at my knees, but not extreme. Just the usual relentless progression of an ordinary osteoarthritis case. I decided to go back to work at what I loved most: medical research. No strenuous activity needed there.

My work as director of the San Diego Clinic Immunological Centre has been the most rewarding I've ever experienced. How could it possibly be otherwise at a facility dedicated to the research and development of products and treatments for ailments for which no current therapy is yet known. And I took advantage of that personally, relentlessly urging more and more research on arthritis. True I had my own interests at stake, but it wasn't hard to justify our efforts, either, not with well over forty million Americans suffering the pain and crippling effects of rheumatoid and osteoarthritis.

Then one day it happened. An obscure little three page article in a pharmaceutical journal was discovered by our researchers. It described investigations made at the US Government National Institutes of Health (NIH) about 25 years earlier. An injectable substance called cetylmyristoleate seemed to possess both preventive and curative properties for laboratory rats with induced arthritis.

We had our doubts. It would surely seem that anything that really worked would have come to light a lot sooner than 25 years. On the other hand, knowing how government agencies like the NIH operate, finding that some important discovery had been buried for a hundred years would not be too surprising.

We decided to give it a try. As interested as I was in treating my own problems, I was even more interested in seeing if it had any benefits when administered orally. After all, it would be far easier to make an oral product available to the millions who need it than make it necessary for them to get prescriptions for an injectable. So I tried taking the foul tasting oil orally. The results: nothing spectacular, but I definitely saw a bit of improvement. Enough to encourage us to develop a product that did work in capsule form for oral administration.

When I took the product that we had developed on our own, which is called CMO, it was like a miracle. I experienced an improvement of about 80% in just a couple of days. Upon repeating the CMO several days later, it was almost like I'd never had arthritis at all. I couldn't believe that my knees, which had been devoid of cartilage and grinding bone on bone for about six years, were now working painlessly and almost perfectly. I could still feel a bit of clicking in my right knee as I walked. And I would get a shot of pain if I twisted a knee joint. But that was heaven compared to what I had been suffering.

Stairs are still a problem for my right knee. Because of the erosion of the bones over the years, they just don't work quite right on the stairs. However, normal flat walking is just fine, and inclined ramps are no longer a problem. I've enjoyed over two and a half years now with no problems and no need for further treatment or medication of any kind. It has set me free sexually as well. Frankly, it has turned my whole life around. I'm no longer a cripple!

It was such a joy, just being able to enjoy a pain-free walk along the beach, or an extended walk through the shopping mall again.

Everybody noticed the difference right away

My daughter lived more than halfway across the country. She only got to see me once or twice a year, sometimes less than that. So it was easy for her to see the changes year by year. It was only a couple of years ago that she reluctantly commented on my trouble walking. But knowing how I hated pity, she never said much more than, "Looks like your arthritis is getting really bad." That was about three years ago. Then, a bit later (as I was carrying her bags at the airport!) she looked at me and squealed, "Dad, you really are cured. You used to just barely hobble around before. I can't believe it. You're walking even faster than I am."

I'm not saying that I can get out there and play football again. But I can hold up to a fair game of fun tennis where we're mostly just lobbing the ball back and forth rather than trying to kill each other. And I still do have a day or two a month as the weather changes that I'm not completely comfortable - just a nagging, dull little ache. (And, I'm happy to say, we've just developed a CMO cream for that, too).

For the most part, though, I'm living a normal active life that's free of the limitations and constant pain that I suffered before we developed CMO. For a disease that conventional pharmacology and medicine can offer only despair, I along with thousands of others who've benefited from CMO, call that a miracle.

NOTE: The San Diego Clinic is dedicated to research and development and patient care. It does not sell or benefit from the sale of CMO or any other product.

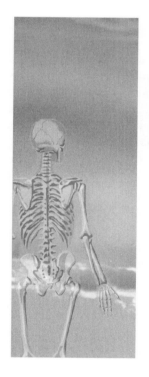

Chapter Six

Who Says There's a Cure for Arthritis?

Who Says There's a Cure for Arthritis?

The effect of CMO is absolutely amazing. Call it a remission, a regression, a relief, a reversal, a remedy, or a cure. Call it what you like, but most patients and even most doctors call it a miracle.

What do the doctors say?

Dr. Douglas Hunt (MD) was so impressed by the results his patients got from CMO that he interviewed several dozen other patients as well, and then decided to write a book about it. In his book, *Boom You're Well*, Dr. Hunt says, "... rheumatoid arthritis damages tissues, causes extreme suffering, and premature death. And so do many of the other diseases that CMO reverses ... If you have rheumatoid arthritis ... then you know I am reporting a miracle ... A MIRACLE."

Dr. William C. Douglass (MD) titled his article about CMO in the newsletter, *Second Opinion*, "A New Miracle Cure for Arthritis" and went on to say, "... now we have a new star on the horizon that promises as much (or more) than the old sure-cures ... This may be the cure we have been looking for ... I think it's worth the investment."

Dr. Mark Muller (DDS) says there's a cure. He knows it for sure, he took it himself. After suffering from osteoarthritis for 30 years, he took just one bottle of CMO capsules. His arthritis disappeared. His pain is gone and he regained full mobility in his rigid neck. His other joints and back, as well, are no longer troubled by arthritis.

You already know about Dr. Sands, Director of the San Diego Clinic, whose detailed experience with CMO was presented in a previous chapter. After several years of crippling bone-grinding-against-bone osteoarthritis in the knees, he is free of pain and has regained over 95% of the mobility in the joints of his knees. Now, three years after taking CMO, and with no further treatment of any kind, he remains fully recovered.

Another doctor reports, "I find CMO absolutely miraculous. It cured my knee problems, which solved my sex problems as well. And it's performing every bit as well for my patients, too."

One of our cases early in 1996 involved a medical doctor, a psychiatrist, who had suffered from almost constant pains in his feet daily for over five years. With CMO those pains disappeared within a day. He has subsequently utilized CMO for many of his patients.

Another of our cases early in 1996 involved a female physician sixty years of age. She suffered relentless pain that resulted from a hip injury about a year earlier. Being a physician, she tried various treatments and medicines that, unfortunately, brought her virtually no relief at all. Finally, she treated herself with CMO and also used massages at the same time to reduce her edema and improve muscle activity. Her pain and inflammation gradually diminished over a period of two weeks. She now remains completely free of pain.

Another medical doctor had suffered from pain and stiffness in his hands for several years. It reached the point where he was no longer able to perform simple office surgery. With CMO he began to feel relief in just one day. His dexterity and fine surgical ability returned gradually over a period of a couple of weeks. He now recommends CMO to his patients.

Yet another medical doctor suffered from osteoarthritis caused by an auto wreck ten years earlier. It had damaged his hip, causing a limp and a severe case of very painful arthritis. CMO relieved his pain permanently in just one day. It was the only relief he found after many years of exploring other possibilities. The damaged hip still causes him to limp, but at least he is now free of pain.

What do the people say?

Mr. G.Y. of Texas writes: "I found out about CMO through a friend ... Even though I really could not afford it, I decided that I had to give it a try.

"I am a 57 year old man. I have had three colon surgeries that left me with only 18" of colon. I had arthritis in my back, hips, and legs. I also had arthritis in my hands and they were always swollen. I had to sleep on my knees in a crouched position because the pain and discomfort of arthritis was driving me crazy. I was really bad off and the doctors told me to get my affairs in order because I didn't have long on this earth. I was willing to try CMO as a last resort. What did I have to lose except the cost of it if it didn't work. This is the result after ... CMO.

"My sleeping has improved by at least 85%. Now I can sleep in any position I want and stretch out on the bed. My arthritis pain and swelling in my hands is gone and there is no more pain in my back, hips or legs. I am also suffering from emphysema and have noticed an improvement, I'd say at least 40%. It seems to be getting better every day. I can walk and do my shopping now and not have to stop every few steps to catch my breath. I have gained back most of my health in more ways than I can explain. CMO seems to be the one thing I needed 10 years ago. I am getting better every day. [Editor's comment: Many people find that the healing process continues long after they finish their CMO capsules.]

"After using the product I can say that it is well worth the cost. I would pay ten times the price if I ever need it again. If you think you can't afford it, think again. For what it does for your body and health, you can't afford not to get it if you really want to be helped. CMO does what it says and much more."

Mrs. R.R. of Michigan, age 41, writes: "All of a sudden, right after my sixth baby, I was struck with terrible disfigurations and joints that kept locking up. I could hardly walk. My doctor said it was degenerative arthritis and fibromyalgia and that there was nothing she could do.

"I was deeply concerned, my grandmother was incapacitated at age 28 with rheumatoid arthritis. And there I was with a new baby and five other children to look after. How was I ever going to cope?

"The pace and degree I was degenerating brought concerns of where I would be in a short period of time. Day by day my fingers were developing growths. My thumbs were extremely painful. My knees, hands and ankles were locking up in growing pain. I was losing the fine motor skills I needed to tend to my family. I dreaded walking. It took me a half hour just to screw up the courage to get out of bed, and I avoided the stairs as much as possible. When I finally did tackle them, I held on to the walls for support.

"My husband worked full time, tended to the children, household chores and laundry. My older children bathed and changed the new baby. The younger children fetched the diapers.

"I also had a sudden twenty pound weight gain after the birth of the baby, which also aggravated my condition. I went to an internist and a rheumatologist with a professional physical therapist. They told me there was nothing they could do to halt the relentless progress of the disease. Except put me on an exercise program, pain killers and steroids. My only hope was to pray and believe in God for a miracle.

"By definition, fibromyalgia often produces insupportable pain, stiffness, and weakness of many important muscles throughout the entire body, plus other symptoms similar to chronic fatigue syndrome as well. For me, the constant pain and the unknown direction of my future tended to bring thoughts of depression.

"Then I happened to hear this radio program - Mark Scott interviewing a medical researcher [Dr Sands] on WXYT in Detroit. They were talking about an amazing new immunological approach to reversing arthritis - with possible benefits for fibromyalgia as well. Something totally new called CMO, a natural immunomodulator.

"I got excited! Was this too good to be true or was it an answer to my prayers? I decided I had everything to gain since my alternative looked so bleak.

"How can I express the joy I now feel, heedlessly scrambling around on the floor with my new baby, or sitting cross-legged and bent over to play - completely free of pain. Yes, free of pain for the first time in eight long months! And I began to feel the difference in just six days.

"Now that I've finished the bottle, my knees don't lock up anymore, my thumbs don't ache, and all my joints move freely and are free of pain. But, you know, one of the greatest benefits of all is to know I can have a quality pain-free life rather than a future racked with pain and plagued with arthritis and fibromyalgia.

"Only if you have been faced with that yourself can you ever know what a relief it can possibly be. My prayer is to see others set free from their crippling pain and difficult existence." [Editor's note: Now, nine months later, Mrs. RR is still enjoying all the same benefits from her one bottle of CMO capsules.]

Mrs. L.M. of New Mexico writes: "Too Good To Be True? That's What I Thought!!!

"Rheumatoid arthritis hit my right knee about 40 years ago, caused from climbing a mountain. Since then, every time I overstressed my knee, it became worse.

"I am now 70 years old and have through the years developed arthritis in my hands and wrist. Also have arthritis as well as scoliosis in my back.

"I love to walk for exercise, but could not do that any more. My wrist and thumbs were so bad I could hardly comb my hair and wait on myself.

"After the fifth day of taking CMO, I was so surprised that the swelling had all gone from my knee and I could rise from my chair much easier, climb stairs, and walk down an incline without the pain.

"It has been one month since I took CMO. My hands are much better and continuing to improve. I wasn't expecting relief for my back, but to my surprise the pain is mostly all gone. Thanks to my friends for introducing me to CMO."

Mr. E.B., age 67, of Michigan reports that his arthritis symptoms first appeared over five years ago and had become a serious problem in his right knee for about two years. His hands were also affected. He writes that his doctor performed an arthroscopy and advised him that his "right knee was bone on bone, but it was not the right time for knee replacement." CMO seemed worth a try.

He is now "lifting weights, ice skating once or twice a week, and getting ready to take a 200 mile bike riding trip. I can now get up ladders and paint. I know this doesn't work for everyone, but I feel it helped me a lot. If my knee never gets worse, I will never think of having a replacement."

Mr J.S. of Texas writes: "In early November of 1996, I was introduced to CMO through the Arthritis Pain Care Centres. The product impressed me so much that it overwhelmed my belief. Knowing that I had arthritis in my hands and elbows and lower back, I was willing to give it a try. Being an avid golf nut, I was willing to try anything that would give me some relief.

"So I did the CMO treatment ... and around the fifth or sixth day, I noticed remarkable improvement in my hands, especially those sore knuckles, and my lower back. By the end of twelve days I noticed that a burning pain from the small of my back down through my leg to my foot was also disappearing. It's now been eight weeks since I finished my treatment and I'm here to tell you that all my pain is gone.

"So golfers, tennis players, softball players and anybody with arthritis pain, do yourself a favour and do the CMO treatment." [Editor's note: Now, over a year later, J.S. reports that he is still golfing vigorously and painlessly as a result of his one set of CMO capsules.]

Mrs M.G., an accountant in California, writes: "My knees have always been a problem, ever since I got hit by a car when I was eight years old. They weren't too bad at first. But when I reached 25 and put on a little weight, they kept getting worse every year. I'm only 38 now, but I've felt like an old lady for the past ten years.

"Now, I can't believe I went dancing! I haven't been able to do that in eight years. I was on my feet, jumping up and down, often on tiptoe, for THREE HOURS at the rock concert! In heels, yet! I haven't been able to wear heels for six years. Unbelievable!

"I overdid it, of course, being out of shape and all. So I got sore muscles but that went away in a day. (You might caution people to take it slow at first. It's so easy to go overboard without the pain.)

"I don't know how to thank you enough for making me feel young again. Who would ever have believed a handful of capsules could do this for me. I swear it's a miracle!" [Editor's note: Mrs M.G. took CMO in August of 1995 and has needed no further treatment of any kind.]

Mr J.P. of Michigan writes: "Though I'm only 36 years old, I had suffered for years with arthritis in my knees as a result of a number of old sports injuries. At the restaurant where I work I often have to get things from the walk-in cooler downstairs, sometimes as much as twenty times a day. The frequent stair climbing is bad enough in itself. Add to that the freezing air from the meat cooler, especially on these cold Michigan winter days, and you've got a killer combination for arthritis.

"I often had to use a knee brace to help me along. Actually, I began to wonder just how long I would be able to hold on to my job before my knees gave out. Well, thanks to you and CMO my knees are just fine now. So much so, I even packed away my knee brace a couple of months ago." [Editor's note: Mr J.P. took CMO in February 1996 and has needed no further treatment to this day.]

Mrs. T.M., age 81, of California sent us a great photo of her smiling beautifully after taking CMO. She had suffered since 1982 with extremely severe pain in her back, shoulder, and knee. She also suffered from sciatica because of a herniated spinal disk [which results in pressure on the sciatic nerve from the inflammation]. She tried various arthritis medications and devices, and though some of them helped, as she put it, "nothing lasted." Her chiropractor couldn't help. She tried Prednisone, Orudis pills, Cortisone creams, BenGay, EMU rub ($56.00 a jar), Capzasin rub, vibrators, heat massage, papain shots, laser treatments, and chelation therapy. None were of any lasting help. Some slowly helped take the pain away by bedtime, "but it was back full blast when I'd wake up." A battery operated device called Alpha Stim ($2600 for three) helped a little.

"However, I was in terrible pain all the time - couldn't sleep. Pain was present always. The pain was severe ... worst in the mornings. Full joint movement was difficult ... affected with knobby lumps. Knee and hands affected with swelling." She took CMO in March 1997 and later in August she reported, "I improved suddenly. The first day there was no pain with CMO. The pain never came back - it's been five months now. I took DHEA and aloe vera plus all the things listed that would help. I got complete freedom from pain ... the very next day after starting the capsules the pain left for good. It's a wonderful blessed relief ..."

She can now walk up and down stairs and inclines, work in her garden, and exercise on her peddler again without pain. "Even after CMO I walk slowly, sometimes unsteadily, and sometimes shuffle a little. But there's no more pain. Dr. Sands was such a big help. Three times when in doubt my husband called and he told us what we should do. [Though other things helped] only CMO gave me 100% relief."

Mrs. J.L., age 65, of Michigan experienced a sudden onset of arthritic symptoms in her hands, shoulders, and hips. In less than a year her fingers became gnarled and twisted out of shape. She wrote, "I'm in pain all the time. My fingers and hands cramp up as well as my feet and legs." She sometimes took as much as 40mg of Prednisone and 100mg of Darvocet, but found them only somewhat helpful. With CMO her fingers straightened so well she sent us before and after pictures. [We regret they're not of publication quality.] Another benefit, her blood pressure dropped from 160/90 to a normal 110/70 - further proof that CMO is an immunomodulator that can normalize a number of different functions within the body. [Editor's note: This normalization of blood pressure is very common in people who take CMO. Specific controlled studies of this effect are being planned.]

Mrs J.M., age 46, of Colorado actually kept a wonderfully detailed day-by-day diary of her success with CMO. Here are some excerpts:

"Problems: Pain and soreness in hip, back, both knees, and left ankle. Arthritic changes due to numerous injuries followed by a number of orthopaedic surgeries. Occupation: Musician/Entertainer. Hobbies: Hiking, horseback riding, bowling, dancing, aerobics, biking. All of these have been virtually impossible without fear of pain for several years.

Day 1, January 8, 1997: Began CMO today. Will be taking enzymes to enhance effectiveness. Suffered a migraine headache ... a terrible one. Wonder if it was due to giving up caffeine?

Day 2: Cleaned house ... really overdid it. Paid dearly for it. Lots of pain in back and hip. Could hardly get around. Sure hope tomorrow is better.

Day 3: Was better today. Got out of bed with very little discomfort. Other times I would have been out of commission for at least two days. Went to town and did a few errands ... was not bothered with pain in my hip or back. My husband and I are entertainers and we do hour long musical shows on Friday nights and twice on Saturday. Usually I am very tired and sore at the end of these shows but tonight went fairly well, and I was not uncomfortable after standing and playing for the entire show. That is a noticeable improvement.

Day 4: Today was a good one. Got out of bed with little or no pain in my hip or back. That's a new one for me as usually it is a struggle. This evening after the show there was a little discomfort, but not nearly as much as usual.

Day 5: Today was another good one ... was not bothered with pain in my hip or back and spent a very comfortable day doing activities that were necessary.

Day 6: Today we went to town and did some necessary errands. Also did some laundry and cleaned a little. By the end of the day I found I had a small amount of pain in my back, but I attribute that to the condition of the road into town. A lot of bumps and ?washboards.'

Day 7: Got up this morning without any discomfort. Have found that I can be comfortable lying on my side during the night; usually I have to move several times ... I had been losing a lot of sleep because of it, and last night I didn't have to take anything to sleep right through.

Day 8: Well this was a pretty good day overall. I am still suffering from a real bad case of the "dumps," but as far as the pain in my back and hip, there was virtually none today. Went into town and did some business, got a few things at the store, and was not bothered by any discomfort. Slept well.

Day 9: Did some laundry, gave myself a facial, and really conditioned my hair. It has been so dry that I feel like a "wild woman" with this mop on my head. After that I went for a walk in the snow. Really enjoyed being out there in the fresh air, and came back without the usual aches and pains I have had before. Also did a few light exercises and was okay with that too. Looks as though this stuff is going to do its job?? Hope the night proves to be another good one.

Day 10: Got up feeling really good. Again slept better than I have in a long time. Went to town, picked up groceries, and did quite a few errands. Then came back ... and made cobbler and biscuits. After that I usually ... take a nap, but today I didn't have time. Did the show without ... pain in either hip or back. Visited with the folks there, came home, and once again had a good night's sleep.

Day 11: Cleaned the house some, did more cobbler and biscuits ... Had a good day. Seems that I am continuing to improve in some way every day. Slept well!

Day 12: Went to Denver to spend the day with family from out of town. After that long a ride I am usually stiff and sore and it takes a while for me to "get moving" again, but today there was no problem. I went bowling for the first time in years, and had no pain during or following three games!!! Before CMO I never would have even considered trying to bowl. I would have been on the sidelines wishing and watching, but today I just said to myself, I'm going to try and see if I can do it. And I did ... WOW!!

Day 13: I really thought that I would be paying for yesterday. I thought after three games of bowling I would be "sitting out" today, doing very little. Guess what, except for a little muscle soreness (normal) everything is great!! Got up and drove my son to the bus at 7:00am. After that, came home and did the dishes and made the bed. We are planning to go and see some friends. This will mean another long ride in the car, and usually I would be dreading that, but today I am looking forward to it. It is a beautiful day! ...

"I want to say thanks to CMO for making such an improvement in my quality of life, and I would highly recommend this product to anyone out there who has similar problems with their health and let it make a lifelong change like no pain medication, diet, or anti-inflammatory has ever been able to do!! NO SIDE EFFECTS. Perhaps in the near future I will venture forth and ride a horse or two. It's about time!!"

Well, we hope we haven't overwhelmed some of you with these rather detailed accounts of CMO users. We do know, however, that we get an enormous number of requests for details of people's experiences. But as we continue relating these experiences we will do so with brief extracts rather than the more lengthy accounts.

Female. Age 45. Arthritis attack worsened rapidly over a period of only seven months. Required a wheelchair to be moved about. Frequently unable to leave bed in mornings because of debilitating pain. Seeking relief, she worked with a personal trainer. She was incapable of holding a five pound weight, unable to make a fist. Saw immediate improvement with CMO in just three days. Two weeks after the first, she took a second course of CMO. She is now able to perform a full workout, has no difficulty making a fist, wakes in the mornings free of pain, and has resumed a normal active life.

Male. Age 32. Rheumatoid arthritis at age 25. Long family history of arthritis. Seven years of pain in hands, shoulders, legs, and ankles. Although subject saw substantial improvement after taking CMO for three days, he did not experience complete relief and continuing remission for about two weeks. He has subsequently enjoyed skiing holidays and has been able to return to playing golf without the discomfort of any pain.

Female. Age 66. Rheumatoid arthritis rendered hands useless, gnarled, inflexible, agonizingly painful more than six years prior to treatment. Pain was relieved and full use of hands restored after five days of CMO.

Adult male. Life-long athlete. Arthritic pain and stiffness in hands, feet, knees, neck, and shoulders - especially severe with exposure to the cold. With three days of CMO, was totally free of pain with dramatically increased articulation in the joints. Further improved mobility came with a repeat set of CMO three weeks later. Since 1995, he now enjoys skiing and other activities with the vigour and delight he lost so many years ago.

Female, age 54. Suffered since 1940 with arthritis in neck, hands, hips, and feet. She was incredulous about the effects of CMO despite reporting that her arthritis was "not affected by the spell of damp, rainy weather for the last two weeks. There's no noticeable hip weakness at all. The tingling and clicking in the pelvic joint is not evident. I'm afraid to believe my arthritis is gone."

Now, in the hope that they will give you a little more insight, here are some very brief extracts from various patients' reports.

... "As gracious as she was about it, still I knew how much of a burden I was on my daughter. That torment of being helpless and encumbering was often even more difficult for me to bear than the pain of my crippled, bedridden body. CMO, what a miracle! It not only liberated my body and my soul, but my daughter as well."

... "It's a miracle! Ten years with arthritis ... three in a wheelchair ... and now I've got a completely normal life again. Just watch me make up for lost time."

... "Imagine my agony. I was a professional athlete all my life. CMO gave me back my life. Even knee surgery didn't do that for me. CMO fixed all my joints, all at once."

... "As crippled as I was, I hadn't worn out a pair of shoes in seven years. Now I'm out shopping for them again - all by myself. My whole life has made a complete about face."

... "After nine years of crippling pain, I can't believe I'm actually skiing again. CMO is truly incredible. I've already told four more people about it."

... "After two years in a wheelchair, I just can't believe that I'm taking care of myself and my family again."

... "I couldn't even put on my own socks. My wife had to do it. Now after seven years of excruciating pain, I'm actually out golfing again."

... "Before, I needed two hands just to lift a cup of coffee. Now I find myself rearranging furniture all by myself. Last week I even changed a flat tire on the car."

... "My arthritis bothered me only when I did heavy work. So I didn't even realize CMO had worked for me till I found myself moving a bunch of heavy junk out of the garage. The change was so smooth and natural I just took it for granted till it dawned on me that I had no more pain."

I am also very pleased to include some letters from Europe that I have received.

Mrs DH, of Gloucester, England wrote ..... "I suffered very badly from osteoarthritis of the lower spine with pain at times so bad I did not wish to go on. After completing the course I can only say that my life is completely turned around. I am so mobile and free from pain it feels like a miracle.I hope this letter will in some way convey the gratitude I feel for having my life back again."

Mrs C, Surrey, England. .... "Before taking the [CMO] I had a problem with BPH, which has improved within a fortnight. I also had a problem with leg cramps from a sciatic nerve injury about 10 years ago. Nothing seemed to work, however after a few days of taking CMO the cramps almost completely went and I can sit cross legged for one hour plus."

Mrs LF, of Kent, England Age 35. "I would like to thank you for your help and support while I was taking CMO."

"After suffering with chronic fatigue syndrome for about thirteen years I spent most of my time resting as I was too tired to manage the most simple tasks, it was like a living death as I have previously been very active. After taking CMO I had a very bad headache and nausea for the first few days but after that I felt much better. I felt relaxed and slept very well I carried on taking the CMO and noticed after doing things around the house I wasn't feeling so tired and this continued. I tested myself by doing a bit more, I even ran across a field which was out of the question before."

"I feel thanks to CMO I have got my life back. I feel young again and things I thought I would never be able to do I'm starting to rediscover, as you know I am planning to marry and thanks to CMO I can look forward to my future. Thanks again."

Mrs M M, Derbyshire, England. "I have nearly finished my first tub [of CMO], and I can tell you that already they are doing me the power of good, it is a miracle. I can now walk without having to use my stick. I am going to order my second bottle and I will keep you posted of my progress."

Ms HM, Cambridgeshire, England. "I started taking the [CMO] at the beginning of October. By the end of the course I had improved quite a lot but still needed as many painkillers. Since Christmas it has taken another spurt. I was able to play snowballing and was able to build a snowman in the beautiful Christmas snowfall. Now after seven years of only being able to take showers, I can get in and out of the bath quite easily. I have not needed to take anti-inflammatories for two months and am now able to cut down on the pain killers.....So many thanks."

Mrs M K, Staffordshire, England. "I have suffered with arthritis for the last two years in my feet and legs - nothing too drastic but enough to curb a lot of my activities, particularly my love of gardening."

"I had a course of Acupuncture last year for about six months, it did halt the pain only left me for a few days after each session. I was told it would need a lot of treatment. I was then told about your treatment and have taken a full course of tablets following a strict diet for recommended. Within a few days I could feel improvement and after the fall course felt more like my old self again. I am now back on my gardening. I am able to do a lot of things I was unable to do last year. I shall always be very grateful to the [CMO] treatment and to all of you that have helped me."

Ms RM, Northamptonshire, England. "I thought I would drop you a short note to say that my feet are much improved after taking [CMO], in spite of being unable to take the tablets without a very small amount of food. Dry oatcakes, seem not to stimulate much reaction."

Mrs MH, Camridgeshire, England. "Thank you for your kind attention, we are absolutely amazed and delighted how [CMO] has worked for my husband. He is driving his car again without any pain. He can walk without his stick and go up and down the stairs no bother, our two sons can't believe the difference in my husband."

Mr DL, Doncaster, England. "I am so delighted with curative effect of the CMO I purchased from you recently, that I am prompted to write to you, and tell you of my experience."

"I have suffered from the most excruciating pain in my right hip, because of osteoarthritis, so bad was the incessant pain, I could not walk 10 yards without pain. As this condition was something I had endured for several years and my doctors could offer only antioxidents and cortisone, and nothing else, I was told the condition was degenerative and that the only hope was a hip replacement operation, to which I agreed and awaited at my local hospital."

"I took the [CMO] capsules more in hope than in confidence in their effectiveness, but after ten days, I felt and indeed deep down inside I knew something very wonderful was happening. After thirty days I had taken my last capsule, and I went to Filey on the East coast in a party of four, and much to my surprise I walked a mile on the sands and on the uneven slippery seaweed covered rocks. After resting on a large rock for 20 minutes I walked back, frequently on a most uneven undulating path."

"I was truly amazed. Although tired when I got back to my car, and I was glad to sit down again. I knew one thing CMO had worked for me!!. I felt cured of the dreaded arthritic condition. I felt like a new man."

"The only thing I can say to Dr Sands and his team of assistants is THANK YOU. I only wish every sufferer could have access to these wonderful CMO, and the sooner the better. For the first time in seven years, I am now pain free."

"When I kept an appointment with a consultant at my local hospital, I told him I was pain free, and he was amazed, and asked me all about CMO. I was pleased to share what I knew with him. And he told me, because I was now pain free, I did not now qualify for a hip operation. How wonderful."

Mr EAC, Troon, Scotland. "I thought that you would like to know how pleased I have been with the results of my course of treatment using CMO capsules."

"Due to injuries to both legs in the Second World War and as a result of having one leg one inch shorter than the other I contracted arthritis in both knees and one big toe. I have just completed the course 100 capsules and only a few days short of the two weeks following the completion. For three weeks now I have felt really good, relaxed, and energetic. My joints are loose and free from stiffness and pain, and particularly noticeable when I have been sitting for fairly long periods and get up to do anything at home."

"My back and at the top of my spine which have given me trouble are now much better and this I regard as a great bonus. Many thanks for your help."

What does the media say?

Newspapers, books, television news, radio talk shows, and medical newsletters all report that CMO is nothing less than a revolutionary breakthrough.

The Mark Scott Show, WXYT Radio in Detroit, provides us with these quotes: "Hang on folks, because if you haven't heard this before, it certainly is going to be an eye-opener for you ... Amazing is not the word for it ... CMO gets to the source of the problem. It actually stops the arthritic process."

The Don Bodenbach Show, KCEO Radio in San Diego gives us these quotes: "It may be what we consider almost a miracle cure for arthritis, and the form of arthritis doesn't matter ... What is more impressive is once you undergo the appropriate treatment ... you are in most cases free from arthritis symptoms forever."

The Nature of Health magazine, September 1996 titled its article, "Stop Arthritis Now! The Amazing Story of CMO" It said, "CMO is a natural substance and is considered an immunomodulator. The reason for the enormous interest is the effect of CMO on both rheumatoid and osteoarthritis ... The results of CMO are so impressive that nothing that mainstream or natural medicine has to offer can come close to the dramatic reversals in arthritis that have been observed ... The link between CMO and arthritis was discovered at the National Institutes of Health ... Standard medical treatment is aimed at symptomatic relief of pain and inflammation and has shown to actually accelerate the disease process ... In contrast, the CMO protocol works rapidly and does not need to be continued in the vast majority of cases."

The *Senior Citizens Reporter* recounts: "CMO is not a conventional product. It's unlike anything that's existed before for arthritis ... it's an immunomodulator, which does not treat the symptoms, but instead corrects the cause of arthritis. CMO acts to normalize or correct the immune function that has gone awry, and that literally halts the arthritic process. Once the destructive process stops the body can heal itself, eliminating inflammation, stiffness, and pain."

The *Military Press* reports: "T-cells incite macrophages to attack the body's own cartilage ... macrophages [are] like garbage collectors inside your body. Their job is to get rid of any foreign matter and organisms they encounter ... and they clean up waste matter as well. That includes any fragments of unhealthy cartilage damaged by some physical trauma or produced by some invading organism like that which causes rheumatic fever ... In the case of arthritis, regardless of whether it's rheumatoid or osteo, once macrophages have dealt with some particles of cartilage they develop a chemical message that's passed on to the memory T-cells ... [which] develop a program instructing more and more macrophages to dispose of more and more cartilage. Unfortunately, that program doesn't distinguish between healthy and unhealthy cartilage. So the onslaught against your joints begins ... CMO acts to normalize the programs in the memory T-cells that are directing the macrophage attacks against the cartilage and the joints. Thus it intervenes in the arthritic process itself regardless of whether it is osteo or rheumatoid. Once the arthritic process is halted and the macrophage attacks are stopped, the body's own healing mechanisms can deal with the inflammation, and its resulting pains soon disappear as well. The effects seem to be permanent."

The *West Coast Jewish News* reports: "CMO successfully intervenes in both the osteo and rheumatoid arthritic process. The proof that CMO is acting as a modulator is demonstrated by the fact that subjects with hypertension [high blood pressure] and others with hypotension [low blood pressure] have both seen their blood pressures normalize as a result of taking CMO. This normalization effect also frequently affects blood sedimentation rates [of lupus patients] as well as insulin requirements in diabetics."

The media in Europe are gradually also waking up to CMO.

In April 2000, *Womans Own*, a British magazine devoted a whole page to the story of eleven year old girl under the title "*I thought only older people got arthritis*". The magazine reports on the wonderful and long lasting improvement this young girl got after CMO therapy.

In Norway, Scandinavia, the top selling and highly respected magazine, *Hjemmet*, reported on its front cover, the sensational headline: "*New natural find removes arthritis*". What followed was a two page spread inside the magazine reporting on CMO, and how a Norwegian school teacher who had to stop teaching as he could not lift his hand because of his arthritis. After CMO therapy, his improvement was such that he could go back to teaching and fishing!

What do animals say?

Apart from meow, woof, moo, baa, oink, squeak, and heehaw, their body language says that CMO is great. In fact, we've never seen a failure with an animal. Absolutely never! Be it horse, dog, cat, goat, hamster, or potbellied pig, we have yet to hear of any arthritic animal that has not responded well to CMO. For more details, refer to the chapter on animals.

One health food store owner told us this funny tale. As he was telling one customer about the wonderful benefits of CMO (98% success rate with his particular clients), another customer who was overhearing the conversation butted in. He related how he had heard one of Dr. Sands' radio interviews and consequently bought CMO for his father. But his father refused to take the capsules, or any other form treatment for that matter.

Now that family also has an old but much-loved dog who, three months earlier, had just sort of given up on things. He just laid himself down by the door and refused to budge from that spot. He ate there, he slept there, and even did all his business there, forcing a rather annoying cleanup job on the family several times a day.

Well, rather than let those costly CMO capsules go to waste, the son decided to give them to the dog. In just a few days, the man said, that dog was up on its feet again and scampering around like it had many years before. But, despite it all, the son complained, he still can't get his father to take the capsules.

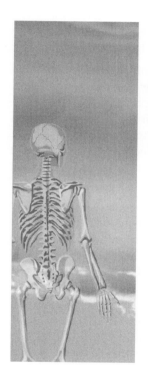

Chapter Seven

Clinically Proved: A Summary of the Clinical Study

Clinically Proved: A Summary of the Clinical Study

This study of 48 persons afflicted with arthritis followed a model prepared by the San Diego Clinic Immunological Centre (SDC). It was not a double blind study. It would not meet the criteria of a formal medical trial conducted for publication by some premier medical journal. But then, that was not its intent.

The objectives of our study were primarily to determine if different types and severities of arthritis would require different dosages. In addition to the information gained directly at SDC, data were compiled from reports from several trusted professional sources that had no vested interest in the results. Data were also received from other medical clinics, medical doctors, osteopathic physicians, chiropractors, physical therapists, and other types of health care practitioners.

The study very clearly accomplished its goals. You may never see it published in the likes of the *Journal of the American Medical Association*. But, as Richard Smith, editor of one of the most prestigious medical publications in the world, *The British Medical Journal*, has unequivocally stated in print, "Only about 15 percent of medical interventions are supported by solid scientific evidence ... This is partly because only one percent of the articles in medical journals are scientifically sound ..." That's quite an admission for a man in his position.

Here then, is a summary of the study conducted over a period of somewhat over seven months in late 1995 and early 1996.

CMO (Cerasomal-cis-9-cetylmyristoleate)
A STUDY ON DOSE EFFECTIVENESS AND PATIENT RESPONSE

The effectiveness and nontoxicity of CMO (cerasomal-cis-9-cetylmyristoleate) arthritis symptoms of pain, inflammation, and impaired mobility having been previously established, the purpose of the present study conducted by the San Diego Clinic was:

1.) to determine optimum dosage levels for various types of arthritis,

2.) to determine if different dosage levels would be required relative to the severity of each type of arthritis,

3.) to observe response time required for initial and partial relief of symptoms,

4.) to observe response time required for complete relief of symptoms, and

5.) to determine factors influencing subjects who may not respond to the protocol.

Subjects were volunteers treated as outpatients. They presented with osteoarthritis, rheumatoid arthritis, and other forms of reactive arthritis.

The study involved 48 subjects. Female subjects (28) ranged from 33 to 82 years of age. Male subjects (20) ranged from 29 to 74 years of age. All races and many ethnic backgrounds were represented. Age, gender, race, and ethnological background appeared to be irrelevant to patient response in this study.

CMO was administered orally in the form of 385mg capsules each morning and evening. The number of capsules and duration of treatment varied for each group of subjects. Subjects were advised to take capsules on an empty stomach with water only; and to avoid tea, chocolate, alcohol, coffee, cola, and other caffeinated drinks for five hours after taking the capsules. Subjects were advised to completely avoid chocolate and alcohol during the entire trial period of two to four weeks duration. With a few exceptions for subjects who could not function without them, steroids were also prohibited. Otherwise diet was not controlled in any way. Subjects were permitted to continue taking their customary pain and non-steroidal anti-inflammatory medications until they were no longer needed. Subjects were asked to visit or call in to report progress at least twice weekly.

Only two subjects failed to show marked or complete relief of all symptoms of pain and limited mobility normally associated with arthritis. Both of these non-responding subjects had suffered prior hepatic problems: one from alcohol abuse resulting in cirrhosis of the liver; the other, a former professional athlete, presented with considerable liver damage from steroid abuse. Further studies are necessary to determine the role of liver function capacity with respect to this protocol. Liver damage resulting from steroids previously prescribed for arthritis may also prove to be a factor affecting patient response.

Two other subjects showed less than a 75% return of articular mobility. The balance of all subjects reported 80% to 100% return of articular mobility as well as a 70% to 100% decrease of pain. Relief of inflammation frequently resulted in at least partial correction of some deformities. Informal independent trials at clinics, by individual medical doctors, and other health practitioners appear to have brought approximately the same results.

MILD TO MODERATELY SEVERE OSTEOARTHRITIS & REACTIVE PSORIATIC ARTHRITIS

In Group #1, eleven subjects presenting with mild to moderately severe osteoarthritis and one with reactive psoriatic arthritis were supplied with 16 capsules, two capsules to be taken each morning and evening for four days. Nine reported about 20% to 30% improvement in articulation and inflammation and about 40% to 50% relief of arthritic pain within 36 hours. In these nine subjects improvement continued rapidly for the next 60 hours, reaching a 70% to 80% overall improvement by the end of the four days. Two of the three latter subjects continued to improve over the following week despite the fact that they were no longer taking the capsules.

However, about half of this group experienced the return of some mild arthritic symptoms after about three to five weeks. (Although not included as part of this study, all of the subjects in this group were treated again and their symptoms have not returned.) The patient with reactive psoriatic arthritis also experienced an almost complete reversal of his associated very severe psoriatic skin condition affecting about 20% of his total skin area.

SEVERE TO CRIPPLING RHEUMATOID ARTHRITIS

In Group #2, nine subjects presenting with severe to crippling rheumatoid arthritis were supplied with 50 capsules to be taken in two series, two capsules each morning and evening for seven days, with a seven day interval before repeating the same dosage for 5½ more days. Four of these subjects were unable to walk and were accustomed to being transported by wheelchairs. One, her femur being fused at the hip, was unable to achieve a sitting position for wheelchair transport. She could, however, move about slowly on crutches as long as she was accompanied by someone to aid her in maintaining her balance. Otherwise she could only stand or lie down. The remaining four could move about with canes or walkers. All nine subjects presented with pain, inflammation, and marked deformation of nearly all proximal interphalangeal and large joints. Five presented with limited lumbar flexion and pain in the vertebral column. All had difficulty grasping and manipulating common objects.

Within three days of treatment six subjects in the group reported a 30% to 50% decrease in pain and 20% to 30% increase in joint mobility, and three subjects reported little change. Within seven days five subjects reported a 70% to 90% decrease in pain and 70% to 80% increase in joint mobility. Three subjects reported to be totally free of pain with almost complete return of joint mobility and marked improvement in joint deformation. One patient reported no perceptible change.

On the fourteenth day, at the end of the one week interval without treatment, six subjects reported minor continuing improvement; two reported maintaining their improved status, and one continued to show no improvement. Treatment was resumed on the fifteenth day for 5½ more days.

By the end of the treatment period all but two subjects reported to be 90% free of pain with return of 70% to 100% mobility. The fused hip joint remained fused, of course, but with a return of over 70% mobility in other joints the subject felt hip surgery now to be worth consideration. The one non-responsive subject proved to have cirrhosis of the liver, which may have been the reason for her inability to respond to treatment.

Further investigation is necessary to determine the role of liver function in this protocol.

MILD TO MODERATELY SEVERE RHEUMATOID ARTHRITIS

In Group #3, fourteen subjects presenting with mild to moderately severe rheumatoid arthritis were supplied with 24 capsules, two capsules to be taken each morning and evening for six days. After three days of treatment eleven reported about 20% to 30% improvement in articulation and inflammation, and about 40% to 50% relief of arthritic pain. In these eleven subjects improvement continued rapidly over the next four days, approaching the 80% to 100% level. The remaining three subjects reported similar improvements by the end of the fourth day, with an overall improvement of 70% to 80% after seven days.

Most of the subjects continued to report minor additional improvement for one week or more even though they were no longer under treatment. However, six in this group began to experience the return of some mild arthritic symptoms after about three to four weeks. (Although not included as part of this study, all of the subjects in this group were treated again and their level of improvement has subsequently stabilized.

SEVERE TO CRIPPLING OSTEOARTHRITIS

In Group #4, fourteen subjects presenting with severe to crippling osteoarthritis were supplied with 50 capsules to be taken in two series, two capsules each morning and evening for seven days, with a seven day interval before repeating the same dosage for 5½ more days. Three of these subjects were unable to walk and were accustomed to being transported by wheelchairs. The other eleven could move about with crutches, walkers, or canes. All presented with pain, inflammation, and marked deformation of nearly all interphalangeal and large joints. Four presented with limited lumbar flexion and pain in the vertebral column. Ten had difficulty grasping and manipulating common objects.

After four days of treatment ten in this group reported 30% to 50% improvement in articulation and inflammation and about 40% to 60% relief of arthritic pain. In these ten subjects improvement continued rapidly over the next three days, reaching 80% to 100% by the end of seven days. One reported no perceptible change.

On the fourteenth day, at the end of the one week interval without treatment, nine subjects reported continuing minor improvement, four reported maintaining their improved status, and one continued to show no improvement. Treatment was resumed on the fifteenth day for 5½ more days.

By the end of the treatment period eleven subjects reported 80% to 100% relief of pain with a return of 80% to 100% mobility. Two subjects reported 70% to 80% return of articular mobility with a 70% to 90% reduction of arthritic pain. The one non-responsive subject proved to have previous liver damage as a result of sports-related steroid abuse. Further studies are necessary to determine the role of liver function in this protocol.

SUMMARY

The results of this study lead to several conclusions regarding its five principal objectives:

1.) Optimum dosage levels appear to be equal for all three types of arthritis investigated: osteoarthritis, rheumatoid arthritis, and reactive psoriatic arthritis. This is evidenced by the gradual return of minor arthritis symptoms in several of those treated with only 16 or 24 capsules, and no regression in those treated with 50 capsules in two series separated by one week without treatment.

2.) Dosage level requirements appear to be equal irrespective of the severity of the subject's condition.

3.) Initial response time for minor improvement appears to vary from two to seven days irrespective of the severity of the subject's condition.

4.) The time for maximum attainable response appears to vary from seven to twenty-one days, resulting in 70% to 100% overall improvement. (Apart from this study, three of the most severely afflicted subjects were treated again after a five week interval, resulting in an additional 10% to 20% overall improvement.)

5.) The two non-responding subjects both proved to have suffered previous damage to the liver from steroid or alcohol abuse, indicating that impaired liver function may preclude success with this protocol.

In addition, it was evident that for many subjects the relief of inflammation resulted in marked improvement in joint deformation.

It is important to note that the substance utilized for oral administration in this study, CMO, was not an unmodified cetylmyristoleate, but the unique form of cetylmyristoleate (cerasomal-cis-9-cetylmyristoleate) - produced using cerasomal techniques to give it a high level of bioavailability when taken orally. Free cetylmyristoleate liquid has very low levels of bioavailabilty orally, and is best utilized only as an injectable.

This study was conducted at the San Diego Clinic, Chula Vista, California, and several additional sites following a model prepared by the San Diego Clinic.

Note: This is the first ever human clinical study conducted, and it was done using only authentic CMO. We have seen promotional literature for other products referring to our study as if it applied to their products. It does not. Any such claim is fraudulent and we do not hesitate to take legal action against such criminal trickery. Please report to us any such dubious claims you may encounter:

San Diego Clinic Immunological Centre

PO Box 121026, Chula Vista CA 91912

Phone: (619) 428-1300

email: immuco@yahoo.com

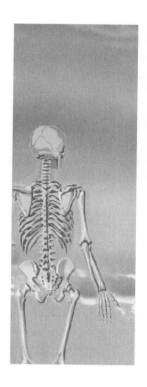

Chapter Eight

The CMO Impostors: Counterfeit and Ineffective

The CMO Impostors: Counterfeit and Ineffective

A Federal Court in California has sent a clear message that it recognizes the authenticity of CMO and will not tolerate the infringement of counterfeiters upon the authentic product.

The United States District Court in Orange, California recently awarded a half million dollars in damages in a judgment against Advanced Labs of Redding, California as a result of a suit filed against them alleging trademark infringement, false advertising, and unfair competition, claiming that those practices resulted in consumer confusion and loss of sales of authentic CMO products.

The CMO mark has been used since November 1995 to clearly and specifically identify the proprietary cerasomal-cis-9-cetylmyristoleate product. CMO is a natural immunomodulator used by people suffering from such ailments as arthritis, Crohn's disease, carpal tunnel syndrome, fibromyalgia, emphysema, migraine headaches, prostate inflammation, and several other ailments with autoimmune involvement.

Advanced Labs had adopted and was using the CMO trademark in its promotional literature and advertising for products of different composition. When Advanced Labs failed to respond to a cease and desist warning letter, the suit was filed against them.

The makers state, "The CMO trademark is distinctive and popular with the consuming public. We have worked long and hard to build up our name and reputation in the healthcare industry, and Advance's actions are causing us to lose customers and sales, as well as seriously damaging our reputation."

"It is grossly unfair for Advanced Labs to position itself in the marketplace through competitive confusion by using the CMO trademark," said W. E. Levin the attorney who filed the suit. Our goal is to permanently enjoin Advance from further violating the trademark rights and to pay for the damage they have done. We hope this sends a clear message to other competitors."

And we say that it's time to clear the deck of products that are misrepresented as CMO, especially since virtually all of them are not only inferior, but ineffective. Many are just scams that take advantage of suffering people by fraudulently using the CMO name.

Although we at SDC have not devoted much energy to tracking down and exposing manufacturers who are fraudulently producing counterfeit CMO, the manufacturer and a number of distributors have been quite persistent in pressing legal action against them. We'd like to present here what some of those investigations found.

The marketplace seems to be sprouting new "CMO" counterfeit impersonators every day. Many consumers, distributors, nutritionists, scientists, physicians, and other health care professionals are confused and dizzy from the spin put on these phony products. We hope to clarify and differentiate between as many of these various fraudulent impostors as best we can. However, this cannot keep up with all the new ones as fast as they appear. Still, you should be able to apply many of the points you find here to other products as well.

First and foremost, let us emphasize that there is only one producer of CMO. It is strictly a proprietary product. There is no other. And it is a totally naturally derived product. As such it contains many beneficial closely related trace substances which aid in its effectiveness - just as the bioflavanoids accompanying vitamin C aid in its effectiveness.

For any product to act as an immunomodulator it must be made of some form of myristoleate. Myristates don't work. And analyses revealed that virtually none of the imitators had even a trace of any form of myristoleate. Some had myristates, which are somewhat similar chemically, but don't work for arthritis. Only one had any cetylmyristoleate at all, and that was in the unaltered form that is very hard to digest and absorb orally.

Our investigations finally led us to issue a brief but comprehensive memo summarizing the various classes of substances being marketed today. We apologize if you find some parts a bit too technical. Here it is:

MEMORANDUM

CMO, CETYLMYRISTOLEATE and CETYLMYRISTATE: A COMPARISON OF PROPERTIES

CETYLMYRISTOLEATE: At room temperature cetylmyristoleate is a liquid wax. It can be digested only in the alkaline environment of the small intestine. Cetylmyristoleate is a large molecule. These molecules have a strong affinity for each other and tend to clump together in large impenetrable masses. This results in a very small surface area relative to its weight and volume. Only the surfaces are exposed to the digestive process. Since that is only a very small percentage of the whole, very little gets digested, giving unaltered cetylmyristoleate a very low level of bioavailability. This is true of virtually all waxes. Faecal analysis indicates that they pass through the digestive system virtually undigested.

CMO: To get an efficient and effective orally administered product, it was essential to raise the digestibility and resultant bioavailability of cetylmyristoleate. Consequently, we had to develop proprietary pharmaceutical processing methods that employ cerasomal technology. The resulting product, now a waxy solid rather than a liquid, was appropriately named cerasomal-cis-9-cetylmyristoleate, and trademarked as CMO.

There is a very important difference between the liquid form and the solid form. As a solid, CMO now resembles a crystalline structure that shatters in the alkaline confines of the small intestine. These shattered particles form a netlike mesh with enormous surface areas, allowing immensely greater digestive efficiency. Furthermore, the reticulated cleavage faces range between 0.9 and 1.0 microns in diameter, which accesses biological uptake mechanisms not available to either larger or smaller particles. Research shows that the body is 40 to 200 times more receptive to particles of this size. This is what makes CMO much more bioavailable and effective than other products. And it is our exclusive proprietary processing methods that make it so.

CETYLMYRISTATE: It's pathetic that we even have to bother with this one. Myristate, as opposed to myristoleate, has virtually no immunomodulatory properties. Thus, it has essentially no effect on arthritis or any other autoimmune disease. The best that promoters of these products (often as cheap as $3.00-$4.00 a bottle wholesale) can come up with to describe their stuff is something like "a free floating myristate." Nobody here can figure out what that means. And the producers won't clarify. If you can figure it out, please clue us in.

A NOTE ON "VEGETABLE" SOURCES: The biochemist's bible, *Baily's Industrial Oil and Fat Products, Fifth Edition, Volume 1, Edible Oil and Fat Products*, clearly lists only four sources for myristoleic acid, the substance needed to produce any form of myristoleate, including cetylmyristoleate. Those sources are beef tallow, butterfat, chicken fat, and sheep tallow. Period! Its extensive listings clearly show that there are NO VEGETABLE SOURCES, not even coconut or soybean oil as some have tried to claim. Any claim that cetylmyristoleate can come from a vegetable source is fraudulent.

A CAUTION ABOUT SYNTHETIC PRODUCTS: Synthetically produced cetylmyristoleate contains a large amount, probably 50%, of trans type cetylmyristoleate. The trans type molecule is unnatural to the body and causes physical damage by disrupting cellular membranes. Even in some so-called "natural" products there remains a trace of toxic residue left from harsh processing. Because it is a completely natural product, CMO has absolutely no trans molecules, and there is no toxic residue because no toxic substances are used in any stage of its processing.

We hope this helps you understand the difference between products, and that there is only one genuine and effective CMO.

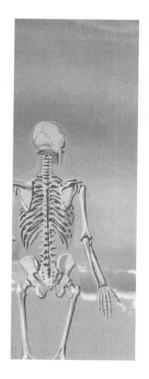

Chapter Nine

Will the Real CMO Please Stand Up?

Will the Real CMO Please Stand Up?

No, the San Diego Clinic (SDC) does not sell CMO. But we know who does. SDC is a research and treatment facility. We are not involved in the sale of any products. We do, of course, dispense CMO to subjects enrolled in our studies, and to clinic patients who may be part of one of our diagnosis and treatment programs for arthritis or other chronic ailments that have autoimmune components.

Since it was SDC that conducted the human clinical studies on CMO, most health care professionals, retail sales outlets, and distributors communicate with us frequently to ask for advice about unusual cases or to report the results of their experiences with CMO. Consequently we know just about all the sources providing authentic CMO and can readily confirm the legitimacy of yours. Simply send us a note or a fax or give us a call:

San Diego Clinic Immunological Centre

PO Box 121026

Chula Vista CA 91912

Phone: 619-428-1300

email: immuco@yahoo.com

Considering how many new CMO counterfeiters seem to crop up every week and how quickly some of them disappear, it is not practical for us to try to compile a list of those counterfeiters to publish here. The list would be out of date by the time this book is off the press.

There are so many impostors, it can be quite a chore trying to decide if the product you've found or are being offered is real CMO or some ineffective imitation. The best you can do on your own is use the information provided in the previous chapter on CMO impostors. Anything that deviates in the slightest from our description of the authentic product should be suspect.

For example, you know that CMO is derived from certain fatty tissue of beef, so that means anything claiming to be derived from a vegetable source couldn't possibly be the authentic product.

You should also be suspicious of products that seem to be priced unusually low. The process for extracting CMO is costly. We've seen many counterfeit products offered at prices lower than it actually takes to produce the authentic CMO. That bargain priced counterfeit CMO is most likely to be nothing more than a waste of your money.

In the previous chapter we presented a copy of a memorandum that describes the differences between CMO and most of the imitation or inferior products. The quality that goes into the manufacture of nutritional products is also very important. The following is a copy of product certification. It presents information relevant to product quality.

PRODUCT CERTIFICATION

Product Designation: CMO

Composition: Cerasomal-cis-9-cetylmyristoleate, a mix of special fatty acids.

Classification: Nutritional supplement.

Import-Export Notice: CMO is a mix of special fatty acids that qualify for import into the European common market and Asian countries by virtue of the processing and manufacturing methods used in its production. CMO is heated several times to super pasteurization temperatures as well as twice subjected to vacuum treatment at pressures greater than that required by

France (as well as some Asian and other European countries) for the import of beef byproducts. The supplier of the raw materials regularly supplies products of all types to France and all of the European common market countries. The product is derived from US beef sources exclusively.

Production: The product is manufactured in a GMP licensed facility according to quality standards defined by the US Government for the production of dietary and nutritional supplements. All production methods conform to Good Manufacturing Practices prescribed by government agency standards.

Agency Inspections: The facility is routinely inspected without notice on a semi-annual basis by Food and Drug Inspectors of the resident state's Department of Health Services according to a schedule controlled by that agency.

Product Source: Natural bovine tallow from US cattle.

Bio-Identification: A free mono-unsaturated fatty acid wax in a mix of related natural tallow-derived waxes.

Melting Point: 34-39°C

Differential Thermal Analysis (DTA): Minimum between 50-60°C with thermogram structure depending on scan rate and packing of sample tube. Matches standards.

Infrared Spectrum: Neat on NaCl plates. Matches standards.

Microbial Testing: Plate count: <10cfu per gram /

E. Coli: Negative. / Salmonella: Negative.

Toxicity: No toxic solvents or other toxic materials are used in the extraction process from its source or in any subsequent processing or handling. Consequently there is no toxic residue in the finished product.

Safety: Closely related fatty acid waxes have for centuries been used in the processing of common foods. They are found in just about every chocolate and natural cheese produced world-wide. They are also commonly used by drug manufacturers in the shells of coated pharmaceutical pills. They are commonly used, as well, in most cosmetics like lipstick and rouge.

Warnings: No product warnings are required. However, as a precautionary measure, it's customary to include the usual text of "Store in a cool dry place out of direct sunlight" and "Keep out of the reach of children" and "Consult your doctor" on any label and as part of any instruction sheet.

Legal History: Since its introduction early in 1995 and use by thousands of consumers, the manufacturer of CMO, its distributors, its dealers, and the medical and other health professionals providing the product have never been sued or otherwise involved in any product litigation. This holds true for any and all other products from the manufacturer as well.

FDA Considerations: CMO is a nutritional supplement. It is derived from natural beef sources as are other common non-prescription products like digestive enzymes and beef liver extract tablets which are freely sold without FDA control. The FDA has never shown any interest in CMO. Just as Cod Liver Oil is a natural product extracted from fish liver, CMO is a natural product derived from certain fatty tissue of US beef.

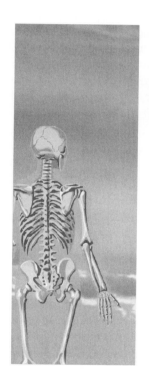

Chapter Ten

Beware the New Drugs!

Beware the New Drugs!

Even more frightening than the ineffective CMO impostors are some of the new drugs now being researched for arthritis. For example, a biotech firm, the Immunex Corporation of Seattle, is trying to resurrect a failed cancer drug and promote its use for arthritis. The company spent billions of dollars developing a drug that turned out to be a total flop for cancer. Now, in an attempt to try to salvage its investment, it is greedily trying to find a way to cram this very dangerous drug into the anti-arthritis category. We find that unconscionable and immoral.

The Wall Street Journal reports, "Scientists are racing to resurrect a set of experimental medicines that figured in one of the most notorious scientific debacles of the biotechnology industry's short history ... The category of drugs largely failed in treating a lethal blood infection. Biotechnology analysts say the success of these new anti-inflammatory medicines is crucial to the industry, which has been in a research slump of late."

The article continues, "Researchers worry that the new treatments will cause long-term side effects, harming patients' immune systems and increasing the risk of contracting other serious diseases. In fact, human tests were recently suspended for one experimental arthritis drug, CE9.1, being developed by IDEC Pharmaceuticals Corporation and SmithKline Beecham PLC. Researchers at those companies encountered worrisome and unexplained immune system effects with the drug."

Worrisome, indeed, because these drugs are immunosuppressants that can impair immune response to attacking microorganisms or the formation of cancerous tumours. Many experts are fearful. "I think we could cure rheumatoid arthritis by using a combination of the new medicines, says Dr. Moreland from Alabama. "The problem is, will you have a viable person left after that?"

Existing immunosuppressants like Methotrexate (also called Rheumatrex) designed for the treatment cancer are altogether too liberally prescribed for arthritis. But it's no wonder doctors get pushed by their desperate patients into prescribing such horrible drugs. The *Physicians' Desk Reference* of pharmaceutical drugs (the doctor's oversized "drug bible") contains 4½ columns of fine-print precautions contraindications, adverse reactions, and warnings about the side effects of Methotrexate. It states, "There is a potential for severe toxic reactions." It is one of the most toxic drugs made. And doctors know it. Yet when suffering patients plead for their doctor to "please, please do something for me," the temptation to prescribe damaging drugs like Methotrexate or cortisone becomes altogether too strong. We've seen livers so badly damaged from Methotrexate and\or cortisone that CMO was completely ineffective for those unfortunate patients.

As an immunosuppressant, Methotrexate also inhibits the action of many of the chemicals that are a vital part of the immune system's defences against invading organisms that cause serious diseases. This is also true of the new drugs from Centocor Inc., Synergen Inc., and Amgen Inc., as well as IDEC. They inhibit the production or action of protective substances like Tumour Necrosis Factor (TNF) and interleukin-1 (IL-1), which could leave a person much more susceptible to cancerous tumours and other diseases, including those caused by invasive viruses and bacteria.

While the arduous process of conventional drug research drags on, the answer is already available in nature. CMO, the natural immunomodulator, already does exactly what those billion dollar projects are looking for. CMO is already clinically proved to be effective against arthritis. It is most important to understand that CMO is not an immune suppressant. Nor is it an immune stimulant. It is an immune modulator. This natural immunomodulator neither suppresses nor stimulates the immune system. It regulates, normalizes, corrects, and controls only those functions within the immune system that have gone amiss.

It does nothing to inhibit proper immune function or response. It acts only on immune programs that have gone awry. That's why, in thousands of patients, it has been shown to have absolutely no negative side effects.

The only 'side effects' so far encountered have been beneficial: lowering high blood pressure, reducing the need for insulin, reducing the inflammation in the lungs of emphysema patients, correcting the blood sedimentation rate of lupus patients, etc. Those are the kinds of 'side effects' doctors love to see.

Moreover, CMO is presented in capsule form to be taken orally. The others, which are drugs rather than naturally derived substances, require either slow hypo- dermic drip infusion or several injections every week. With CMO, however, the benefits seem to be permanent or, at least, long lasting. Once the faulty immune programs are normalized, they seem to stay that way.

Furthermore, CMO works for osteoarthritis as well as rheumatoid. (What those multi-million-dollar scientists don't seem to realize yet is that evidence suggests that autoimmune misprogramming is involved in just about all types of arthritis.)

Considering the success of CMO in its clinical study, the extraordinary results in practical use by physicians, the absence of side effects, success with thousands of users, and its immediate availability to the public, CMO certainly warrants serious consideration as an option for anyone with arthritis.

Try it. It does more than stop the pain. It stops the destruction of your joints as well. Try it. You'll wish you'd done it sooner.

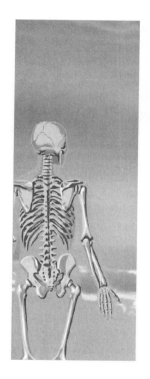

Chapter Eleven

CMO and Other Ailments

CMO and Other Ailments

How is it, people ask, that CMO can be of benefit for so many different ailments? To understand it, think of penicillin and how many different kinds of infections that general antibiotic cures. It has turned out that CMO is so much more than just an arthritis remedy. It is a general immunomodulator that has proved beneficial for nearly any ailment that has any autoimmune factors involved. And there are dozens of them. We're talking about ailments like:

Fibromyalgia, emphysema and asthma, Crohn's disease, prostate inflammation, lupus erythematosus, ankylosing spondylitis, Psoriasis, carpal tunnel syndrome, Sjögren's syndrome, scleroderma, TMJ, neck, back, and foot pain, Behçet's syndrome, macular degeneration, tension headaches, migraine headaches, cluster headaches, Reiter's syndrome, myasthenia gravis, hypertension, sarcoidosis, sciatica, tendinitis, tennis elbow, diabetes, even multiple sclerosis, bursitis ... and more.

And those are just the ones we have specifically heard something about. Yet, for a long while, we were very reluctant to discuss any diseases other than arthritis. We had no formal studies for them. And we were concerned about credibility. We were not about to take the irresponsible position of recommending CMO for ailments on which we had so little data, despite reports of having literally saved several patients from certain death and a few others from suicide.

Initially, we didn't have an inkling that CMO would prove to be valuable for ailments other than arthritis. The tiny journal article describing the discovery at the National Institutes of Health spoke only of a mouse study related only to arthritis. We examined that study, did some preliminary explorations, and then conducted our human clinical study, but only for arthritis. That's all we knew. But we were soon to learn that a great number of other ailments with autoimmune factors as part of their makeup would also respond favourably with CMO.

The first hint we got that it might benefit other ailments came when we received a phone call from one of the first physicians using CMO regularly in his arthritis protocol. In a rather puzzled voice he asked, "What effect does CMO have on emphysema?"

We were stumped, so we decided to put the ball back in his court and responded with, "Why do you ask?" The doctor went on to explain that he saw a dramatic and measurable improvement (about 40%) in the lung capacity of an emphysema patient after treating her with CMO for her arthritis.

When we replied that we had no experience or data regarding CMO and emphysema, he asked if we thought it might help another patient with severe emphysema. We explained that we didn't know, but we didn't see how our nontoxic natural substance could do any harm. So the doctor decided to try it.

The patient had been on oxygen 24 hours a day for nearly two years and she left her bed only to go to the bathroom and to have dinner with her family a couple times a week. Amazingly, after five days of CMO she was breathing so well she no longer needed oxygen, and a week after that she was out driving around doing her own shopping again. We were all astounded!

Marie, a great grandmother now in her eighties, is another perfect example of multiple benefits. She took CMO for her arthritis long before we had any idea it could help her emphysema as well. Her arthritis was so severe a good night's sleep was next to impossible. And that brought on tension headaches that would greet her every morning.

She had suffered for years with emphysema. During her next regular checkup her doctor was amazed by the fact her arthritis seemed to have disappeared. But he was even more surprised when her x-rays showed a dramatic change in her lungs. The emphysema was in remission. Her breathing was the best it had been in several years.

There had been still another problem. Over the past five years she had been rushed to the hospital several times with her tongue so swollen she couldn't swallow. Each time the emergency room staff treated it as an allergic reaction to food, probably citrus. Her doctor prescribed various medications but the attacks continued. Now, two years after her one time treatment with CMO, she's never had another attack — even though she discontinued all the prescribed medications long ago. So here's a case where CMO not only cured her arthritis, but her emphysema, her headaches, and her citrus sensitivity as well. She has recently ordered another bottle of CMO as a safeguard. She never wants to suffer like that again.

Still, it was a puzzle how CMO was affecting emphysema. We know the chronic inflammatory process in emphysema can swell lung tissue. The irritation can also causes fluid to seep into the areola (spaces) where oxygen is absorbed. Both the swelling and the fluids reduce a lung's capacity to absorb oxygen from the air. Almost all chronic (long-duration) ailments do develop autoimmune factors. We finally concluded that CMO, as an autoimmune modulator, was probably intervening in the inflammatory process and reducing both the swelling and the seepage. Chronic inflammation is a significant factor in emphysema patients.

It was only a few days later that we received the same kind of inquiry from another doctor about systemic lupus erythematosus. Well, we know that lupus definitely has autoimmune components. In fact it's sometimes classified as an "allied rheumatic disorder" or as a "connective tissue disease." However, lupus is very difficult to treat. Even antimalarials and intravenous steroids often bring only little relief. So we were surprised at the splendid results the doctor got with CMO. We have since received other favourable reports. We kept getting similar reports regarding one disease after another, and soon it became obvious that CMO is a general immunomodulator that could benefit just about any ailment with autoimmune factors.

Initially we were very reluctant to discuss how CMO benefited other diseases. We were concerned about credibility. We were already battling the "charlatanism" attitude over arthritis alone. Most conventional doctors are resistant to change. We didn't want CMO to take on the character of some old medicine peddler's snake oil — "a cure for everything that ails you." That could harm our credibility more than ever.

And, of course, it's not a cure-all. But we do look forward to the day when formal CMO clinical studies for these other diseases can be made. It will also be equally interesting to see how well CMO functions in combination with other therapies against many other ailments.

Now let's look at how CMO may specifically be of benefit to some of these other ailments individually. (Check the index regarding any ailment for which you may want to find information quickly.)

You're now about to read about a great number of so-called "incurable" diseases.

Fibromyalgia and Scleroderma

The history of one typical success of CMO for fibromyalgia is detailed in the personal report from Mrs R.R. of Michigan. You can read how she conquered this "incurable" disease on page 69.

Like arthritis, fibromyalgia is probably triggered long before the symptoms become obvious. Still, especially with fibromyalgia, those symptoms may become very severe in a very short time. The advanced symptoms include muscular weakness affecting many major muscles, persistent joint and muscle pain, stiffness that is hard to eliminate, joints that frequently lock up, and debilitating chronic fatigue.

Often, knobby growths appear on the fingers as well. Clumsiness sets in as motor control diminishes.

It's another one of those "incurable" diseases that leads your doctor to say, "Sorry, there's nothing more we can do." And if you're a severe case you get sent home to wait for the inevitable deterioration of your body that eventually leads to insupportable pain and a wheelchair existence. Depression and suicide are not uncommon.

Mrs R.R., at age 41, had already been told there was nothing more that could be done other than exercise and physical therapy. But with just one bottle of CMO she was able to get free of pain, regain her strength, resume her household chores, and scamper around on the floor with her baby.

Another woman in her eighties complained that her pain was so bad she hadn't had a decent rest in over two years. She was never able to sleep more than two hours at a time and rarely got more than three or fours hours during any night.

She suffered the customary pains and weakness, complaining mostly about her hands and knees. She couldn't even hold a pen for more than a minute. After just three days on

130

CMO she was sleeping comfortably again. Within a week she was free of pain. Her hands and legs regained their strength and she resumed her normal activities, including letter writing with a pen.

Though we don't see quite as high a success rate with fibromyalgia as we do with arthritis (probably about 70% to 75%), we're working on bettering those results.

Scleroderma responds in a manner quite similar to fibromyalgia. However, the success rate of CMO for scleroderma is even a bit lower than that for fibromyalgia. Nevertheless, we are getting a number of good CMO success stories for scleroderma too.

Emphysema and Sarcoidosis

We talked about emphysema quite a bit already at the beginning of this chapter. This lung disorder also goes by the name of Chronic Obstructive Pulmonary Disease (COPD). It reduces the lung's capacity to assimilate oxygen. The ailment is usually associated with smoking, but it can also be caused by prolonged exposure to smog, vapours, dust, or other contaminants in the air of environmental or work conditions.

The expansion and compression of gasses by persons who are professional scuba or commercial divers can also lead to this disorder. If you're in it just for the sport, don't worry. You're probably not diving frequently enough to develop the problem

It's not an ailment that receives a lot of attention publicly, but it's a killer. It ranks fifth in the cause of death in the US, and even higher in countries where smoking is even more common.

The recovery of the first patient described at the beginning of this chapter was truly remarkable. She got off oxygen in just five days after needing it 24 hours a day for two years. Then just a week later she was out driving around shopping again. Very dramatic yes, but it's not unique. Most emphysema victims we encounter are not so severely affected, but we've heard of many, many cases and virtually all of them have responded exceptionally well.

Sarcoidosis

Although the granule-like lesions of sarcoidosis are most frequently found in the lungs, they may also develop in the heart, liver, spleen, muscles, and bones. The ailment seems to have some strong autoimmune components. The only case treated with CMO responded very well, relieving pain and inflammation and restoring normal function to the affected areas.

Asthma

Asthma is a different matter. Although it is a chronic inflammatory disease of the airway, patients respond in unpredictable ways to CMO. Some respond well but others actually worsen.

Asthma is often divided into two basic categories: intrinsic and extrinsic. The intrinsic type is a straightforward reaction to things like irritating substances, infection, cold air, exercise, emotional upset, etc. The extrinsic type involves an immune reaction to pollen or other substances to which the asthmatic is allergic or sensitive.

Unfortunately there's no telling how either type will respond to CMO, so we recommend that its use always be managed by a physician. We also suggest that initial doses be very small, perhaps only one capsule daily for a couple of days with increases by an additional capsule per day every other day. No one is likely to run into serious trouble that way. Any indication of sensitivity should be immediately discussed with your physician. CMO should be taken in divided doses, half in the morning and half in the evening. Once a dosage totalling six capsules daily is reached it should be maintained at that level.

Prostate inflammation

When there's no infection or cancer involved, it's called Benign Prostatic Hyperplasia (BPH). The swollen prostate gland puts a lot of pressure on the urinary bladder and reduces its ability to hold normal amounts of urine. The first sign of BPH is the need to urinate very frequently. Often, urinary incontinence follows. BPH may also cause discomfort during sexual activity, reducing the sex drive. The pressure on the seminal vesicles may also block the flow of sperm to the seminal fluid causing the ejaculate to be infertile. Often there are feelings of pressure in the lower abdomen, sometimes accompanied by pain.

Surgery is one option. Medicinal and nutritional therapies can help somewhat, but nothing seems to achieve the simple and dramatic results we often see with CMO. We've seen patients' symptoms disappear in less than a week. And it all happens without the dangers and negative side effects of prescription medications.

Some patients take longer, of course, but once the inflammation is relieved, interest in sexual activity normally returns. This is in such sharp contrast to the impotence which so frequently occurs after surgery. The prostate plays an important role in sexual function. Sexuality is frequently altered or completely destroyed by prostate removal. By contrast, CMO leaves the prostate intact, and there have been many reports that it actually stimulates the sexual drive. A few patients swear that it's an aphrodisiac and that it has improved their performance as well as their desire. A few doctors have also confirmed such reports.

One man reported relief of his swollen prostate symptoms within a week and that his sexual activity increased from near zero to twice daily. His medical exam confirmed the reduction of prostate inflammation and his cheerful attitude confirmed the other. Those results are quite common with CMO.

Another man who found relief from his prostate inflammation also reported finding sex to be a totally new and pleasurably exciting experience. He wants to explore the possibility of using CMO in small doses on a continuing basis to see if his heightened pleasures persist. So far, so good — but we must await the long term results before reaching any conclusions.

Sometimes prostate inflammation is caused by bacterial or viral infections. That's called prostatitis and should not be treated with CMO alone. Antibiotics or antivirals should be used as well to defeat the infecting organisms. CMO can help with the inflammation, but the medicines are necessary for infections.

Lupus erythematosus

Here's another "incurable" disease that usually responds well to CMO. Systemic lupus erythematosus (SLE) is often considered to be a condition in the arthritis family — an inflammatory connective tissue disorder. Unfortunately it can also involve the liver, kidneys, blood, skin rashes, and central nervous system. It is unquestionably an autoimmune disease, and after hearing so many glowing reports of CMO's effectiveness early on, we expected it to make a major impact on this disease. Many lupus patients respond well with CMO, yet some do not. We still have not found out why that's so, but we're working on it. As I keep saying, we have so much more to learn about this marvellous substance.

Lupus was one of the very first diseases that gave us a clue that CMO is a general immunomodulator that could benefit autoimmune ailments other than arthritis. From the very beginning we kept hearing how it relieved so many of the painful symptoms and how it normalized even extremely high blood sedimentation rates.

One male patient in his fifties is a typical example. He suffered with debilitating fatigue, joint and muscle pains, muscular weakness, kidney pains, urinary bladder control, and sleeplessness.

For over ten years his disease became progressively worse. Conventional medications were of little help. Turning to a holistic doctor (Dr Douglas Hunt, MD) for help, he was put on CMO along with a few other nutritional supplements. CMO combined with type two collagen, manganese, proline, and vitamin injections turned his health around in just a few weeks. Melatonin took care of the sleeping problem.

His aches and pains disappeared and his energy levels improved rapidly. He regained muscle strength and control of his urinary bladder. Naturally, his outlook on life brightened considerably as well.

But, unlike overcoming arthritis, this wasn't a one-shot deal. Continuing treatment seems to be necessary to keep him in remission. And we are finding that continuing treatment may be essential to conquering other "incurable" ailments as well. But that doesn't necessarily mean taking CMO every day. Often just a few capsules once or twice a week are quite enough, sometimes along with conventional medications as well.

Multiple Sclerosis

Multiple Sclerosis (MS) has long been one of the most difficult and challenging diseases for medical science. It is so frequently relentless in its degeneration of virtually all body functions, and is often stubbornly unresponsive to conventional treatment. Despite the fact that MS clearly is a chronic ailment with autoimmune components, we never expected that this degenerative disease would respond to CMO. Yet, in many cases it definitely has.

One of our most current reports concerns Mrs J.V., an emergency room nurse who recently decided to try adding CMO to her treatment protocol. In 1966 she experienced a numbing weakness in her left leg along with some trouble keeping her balance. Doctors diagnosed it as a mild stoke. She is now sure it was an early sign of MS. Within a few years the numbness below the waist became more generalized and was accompanied by tingling sensations. That's when doctors began to suspect MS.

The disease gradually worsened over the years. Her left leg began to drag and the lower body numbness worsened. She had virtually no balance, suffered from constant dizziness and eye spasms. At best, she could walk only a dozen steps unaided and when fatigued, not at all. She lacked the strength and balance to pick things up from the floor. To manage a flight of stairs, she often had to crawl up the steps one by one.

After an MRI several years ago finally and clearly established that she had MS, the doctors prescribed medications with such serious side effects that she refused to take them. She chose a milder one and put herself on a healthy vitamin program instead. Then a friend told her about CMO. Taking an immunomodulator for an autoimmune disease like MS made great sense to her and she promptly added it to her therapy along with some colloidal minerals.

For a few days on CMO her energy levels varied. But after the fifth day they continued to rise and she now leads a perfectly normal life. Her business associates comment on the remarkable change. CMO has turned her life around. "It's so wonderful," she says, "just to walk through a mall again."

Incidentally, the arthritis in her hands has disappeared as well. But that's no surprise.

She has recommended CMO to several others also suffering from MS. Their responses have been excellent. One friend, who literally spent at least 20 hours a day in bed, returned to normal in just three days after adding CMO to her therapy.

We also have a report of another female, age 52, who was suffering with a slowly progressing MS for over ten years. Though she experienced occasional flare-ups, her main problem was muscular weakness, fatigue, lack of endurance, and depression. CMO cleared up these symptoms in less than a week. She can now walk twice as far for her morning exercise. She, too, is now able to do her housework again for the first time in years.

Another MS patient complained that after a year in a wheelchair he was stiffening up. It was taking longer and longer to get through his daily routine. He was amazed how CMO restored his physical strength. His sex drive also jumped from zero to well above normal. He seemed to be just as pleased with that as anything. Unfortunately, irreversible nerve damage still keeps him confined to the wheelchair.

We have also received a few reports where CMO provided only the minimal benefits of easing the pain of MS patients. One factor in MS is autoimmune destruction of the myelin sheathing that covers the nerves. It's like a mouse chewing away the insulation of an electrical wire. The exposed nerves become very sensitive and painful. In this case, perhaps CMO is halting that particular process and allowing regeneration of the protective myelin sheathing. We suspect CMO is intervening in other destructive processes as well.

There remains the need for a great deal of exploration regarding CMO. A number of MS cases have required maintenance doses of CMO to sustain its effectiveness. There is also a need to explore the use of CMO in conjunction with other medications and nutritional supplements.

Substances that are likely to work well along with CMO are superoxide dismutase (SOD) and glutathione as well as other antioxidants. Relatively high doses are probably appropriate during any flare-ups. Fish oils and flaxseed oils may also be helpful.

It is unwise to discontinue other therapies while using CMO for MS. CMO appears to be compatible with virtually all other therapies. Consult your physician!

The very latest findings reveal that the HHV-6 virus is the likely precipitating cause of MS. But defeating that virus is not likely to be the whole answer. The autoimmune processes that have been programmed into the Memory T-cells will probably have to be corrected as well. CMO is the best solution for that.

Psoriasis and psoriatic arthritis

We've dealt with psoriatic arthritis earlier in the book. It responds just as well to CMO as any other form of arthritis. But recently we have been surprised by numerous reports of improvements in the dermatological outbreaks as well. Many patients have seen dramatic improvement, some reporting complete disappearance of the rashy outbreaks. Future study may prove CMO to be of benefit in controlling psoriasis even when no arthritic symptoms are present. Mrs J.V., the multiple sclerosis patient whose case history is given above, had a patch of psoriasis on her scalp disappear completely with her CMO treatment.

Crohn's disease, ulcerative colitis, irritable bowel, diverticulitis, Sjögren's syndrome, Behçet's syndrome, Reiter's syndrome, etc

Many gastrointestinal diseases respond promptly and extremely well to CMO. Crohn's disease, colitis, diverticulitis, irritable bowel, etc, all involve chronic inflammatory processes that are readily influenced by CMO. However, some problems, like ulcers, need special attention. And for these gastrointestinal diseases we do, when necessary, make exceptions to the "empty stomach" rule. If CMO is not well tolerated because of digestive difficulties, it's better to take it along with a little light food.

Crohn's disease (also known as transmural colitis or granulomatous colitis) has in practically all cases responded fully to CMO. Just what causes the inflammation of the large and/or small intestine remains a medical mystery. Apart from certain foods, stress is considered to be a major trigger factor. There are probably also genetic factors involved.

Though its symptoms are frequently treatable, many do not respond well. There seems to be no permanent solution to this recurring chronic problem available through conventional medicines. CMO, on the other hand, has almost always been able to provide permanent relief with just one set of capsules for a multitude of patients. Nevertheless, a few patients have needed to continue taking a couple of capsules now and then when they feel a flare-up may be coming on.

The most frequent symptoms are abdominal cramping and pain, excessive intestinal gas, diarrhea, and occasional fever. These are often brought on by food irritations. Severe cases can result in perforation of the colon and rectal problems or bleeding. CMO usually brings relief within a week. It has been as successful with severe cases as with mild ones, although it may take more than one bottle. If complete relief is not obtained, just keep a bottle of CMO handy and take two or three capsules the moment you detect any signs of a flare-up.

Ulcerative colitis can be very serious and require hospitalization for severe episodes. The most telltale sign of this disease is frequent bloody diarrhea or bloody mucosal discharge. Pain, cramping, and tenderness usually occurs in the left colon. Weight loss and anaemia are frequent complications. Fever may indicate infection.

Because of its effects against the autoimmune inflammatory process, CMO (taken with a bit of food) has often been quite effective against this ailment. When cortisone has been prescribed it should not be discontinued until the ailment has been resolved. You should definitely seek medical supervision for this problem.

Diverticulitis patients usually suffer from the same lower left abdomen tenderness, intestinal pain and cramping, constipation or diarrhea, and autoimmune inflammation that appears with ulcerative colitis. Diverticulitis appears more often with advancing age. Perforation of the colon may also occur in severe cases.

Treatment with CMO usually brings good results, often all by itself without other therapy. Nevertheless, it would probably be best to continue any conventional therapy with medical supervision until the problem is completely resolved.

Irritable bowel syndrome is the catch-all label put on any number of common bowel disorders of unknown cause. CMO has been very effective in eliminating most of these complaints.

Sjögren's syndrome, when it appears, usually does so in patients suffering with arthritis and related conditions like fibromyalgia, scleroderma, lupus, etc. The most common symptoms are dryness of the eyes and mouth. The nose, throat, larynx, bronchi, skin, and vagina may also be affected. Errant autoimmune attacks occur against the tear, salivary, and thyroid glands — and sometimes even RNA. Serious problems with scratchy eyes, speaking, and swallowing food often develop.

The best conventional medicine has to offer for Sjögren's sufferers is an artificial tear formula, mouth moisteners, skin creams, and vaginal lubricants. Our reports indicate that CMO has been very successful in conquering this ailment.

Behçet's Syndrome is a chronic inflammatory disease that may be dormant for years and years, or may produce many serious complications. Painful ulcers of the mouth, penis, scrotum, vulva, and vagina are common. The eyes may also be affected. Hazy vision or blindness may result. Steroids are about the only treatments that are employed conventionally.

This disease is quite rare in the US and we have feedback regarding only two cases. CMO was quite successful with one and the other was helped somewhat. In both cases steroids were not discontinued while taking CMO, but so far the one who responded well no longer needs them.

Reiter's syndrome is a complicated disease with autoimmune components more commonly found in young males rather than mature men. It is often triggered by sexual intercourse, chlamydial infection, and/or bacterial diarrhea. Frequently a combination of clinical manifestations appear: arthritis, urethritis, conjunctivitis, uveitis, and mucosal tissue infections or disturbances. Successful treatment usually requires the use of conventional therapy along with CMO, although use of steroids should be minimal.

Myasthenia gravis

Myasthenia gravis is a neuromuscular disorder affecting the voluntarily controlled muscles. Weakness and rapid fatigue may range from mild to completely debilitating. It may even become life threatening. The muscles involving speech and swallowing may also be affected. It is believed to be caused by autoimmune problems that degrade or block acetylcholine receptors of muscular nerves. It is frequently associated with disturbances of thymus gland function. Removal of the gland is sometimes suggested, but may possibly be avoided by using CMO.

In order to recover her energy, the wife of one doctor needed to rest for an hour or more after just twenty to thirty minutes of very light activity. Her strength and stamina returned to just about normal after adding CMO to her conventional non-steroidal treatment. However, she did require small maintenance doses of CMO two or three times weekly to sustain her level of improvement.

The administration of CMO along with conventional medications should be carefully monitored by the primary care physician on the case. There are an ample number of non-steroidal medications that may be used with CMO.

Diabetes

Diabetes was another early puzzler. Many physicians began reporting that diabetic patients taking CMO for arthritis were requiring less insulin. I checked into that mystery personally and found that a substantial percentage of diabetics suffer from autoimmune destruction of the pancreatic cells that produce insulin. It seemed reasonable to conclude that CMO was intervening in those attacks, saving the insulin-producing cells from destruction and allowing the generation of new cells to continue undisturbed.

Although vitamin E does not help pancreatic cells produce more insulin, daily use is known to reduce plasma glucose, triglycerides, free fatty acids, and cholesterol. It has been suggested that the use of vanadyl sulphate can greatly improve the effectiveness of insulin.

Studies are needed to determine if a protocol for the effective treatment of diabetes using CMO can be developed. We would welcome the participation of other clinics and physicians.

Macular degeneration and diabetic retinopathy

Macular degeneration is the leading cause of blindness in persons over 65 years of age in the USA. It starts with a thickening of certain fibres in the eye and deterioration of the capillaries of the blood supply. Detachment of the pigmented layers of the eye may occur eventually. Total blindness or loss of central vision may result.

Diabetic retinopathy is the leading cause of blindness in adults from 20 to 65 years of age in the USA. It involves dilation and bleeding of the veins in the retina which can also lead to retinal detachment.

These ailments are often associated with diabetes, hypertension, sarcoidosis, toxoplasmosis, or syphilis. Corrective surgery, often by laser, is very costly but frequently recommended as the only conventional therapy. Most cases treated with CMO have responded exceptionally well, eliminating the need for surgery.

Just what autoimmune processes, if any, are being affected by CMO in these diseases has yet to be determined. We have so much more to learn about the secret mechanisms of CMO and its broad range of influence on so many ailments.

Migraine, cluster, vascular, and tension headaches

Migraine and vascular headaches are caused by the dilation, distention, and inflammation of the branches of the carotid artery. They are often throbbing headaches affecting the areas behind the eyes. They may be accompanied by nausea or vomiting, moodiness, depression, irritability, and visual disturbances. They may also be caused by eating or inhaling toxic or irritating substances.

Cluster headaches come suddenly, are severe but of short duration, and tend to recur several times in a day. They usually affect only one side of the head near the eyes, but may radiate to the temple, nose, jaw, and neck. They can cause reddening of the eyes, tearing and nasal stuffiness. They may be caused by allergies or chemical sensitivities and temporary relief can often be achieved using antihistamines.

Tension headaches are usually caused by tension or spasms in the muscles of the neck and shoulders. They are an occupational hazard of desk-bound employees, dentists, chiropractors, carpenters, and others forced to remain in awkward positions for long intervals.

Migraine, vascular, and tension headaches usually respond well to CMO because of the chronic inflammatory processes involved. Cluster headaches that are normally relived by antihistamines often respond even better when CMO is added to the therapy. CMO may even help reduce the number of recurrences per day.

Hypertension (high blood pressure)

How on earth could CMO affect high blood pressure? That was also one of our earliest puzzlers. We were getting dozens of reports of blood pressure normalizing after CMO treatment for arthritis. At first we thought maybe because CMO brought about the release of the anxiety as well as the physical pain and aggravation of arthritis, patients were just more relaxed. That could help bring blood pressure down.

But we soon found that patients with very mild cases of arthritis but severe hypertension problems were also seeing their blood pressure normalize. Certainly knocking the arthritis out of someone's big toe isn't going to bring that much of an emotional change. So there must be something else going on.

Of course there already are plenty of good medications for hypertension. But they all have side effects that can build up to dangerous levels after prolonged use. And often, higher and higher doses of even stronger medications are needed as tolerance to the meds builds up. Liver or kidney damage is not uncommon. It would also be just as valuable in hypertension as it is in arthritis to be able to treat the cause rather than just the symptoms. So a nice nontoxic and possibly permanent solution like CMO could be welcomed as new ammunition against hypertension. We decided it was worthwhile looking for the answers.

We concluded that the major factor may be the stiffening of the endothelial lining (the inner surface) of arteries and veins. Blood vessels must be flexible to allow the free flow of the pulses of blood pumped out by the heart. That's what you feel when you count your heartbeat by taking your pulse. If the blood vessels are stiff, they hinder the flow of blood and the pressure builds up within them.

Drugs are not known to restore endothelial flexibility, but we are quite convinced that CMO does. We have yet to prove it, but we're confident that in time we will discover the mechanism by which that happens.

Regardless, we have reports of many cases of reversals of hypertension by CMO, with and without the simultaneous use of conventional medications. CMO seems to be compatible with all heart and hypertension medicines. In fact, we've even heard of heart murmurs and irregular heartbeat disappearing after taking CMO.

Controlling hypertension, of course, plays a role in reducing the likelihood of heart problems as well.

One patient who was given CMO for arthritis in his knees had his high blood pressure normalize almost immediately. After using CMO, he reported that he hadn't needed his hypertension medication in weeks. And, of course, his knees got better, too.

Mrs J.V., the MS patient, found that her high blood pressure dropped a full 60 points upon completing her treatment with CMO. Another patient had systolic blood pressure surges that sometimes topped 200. Experimenting with various conventional medications and altering their doses brought no relief. A long program using CMO, coenzyme Q-10, taurine, fish oils, and minerals along with his normal medication gradually brought the hypertension down to acceptable levels.

Antioxidants like superoxide dismutase (SOD) and glutathione may also enhance the relaxing effects on the endothelial lining.

Sciatica, low back pain, ankylosing spondylitis

The sciatic nerves radiate down the buttocks and legs. Strains, sprains, pinched nerves and arthritis can send awful pains shooting along these nerves or even persist to a paralysing degree. The slightest movement can sometimes generate feelings like a knife has been plunged into the area.

Back pains are the second leading cause of doctor visits for adults over 45 years of age. If they're caused by arthritis or chronic inflammation in the back or spine, CMO is very likely to help.

As we have discussed in great detail in earlier parts of this book, CMO will almost always correct the problems that cause neck, back, leg, knee, and foot pains. That also holds true for ankylosing spondylitis and the chronic inflammation caused by injured or dislocated spinal disks. In some cases, though, surgery may be necessary to correct some structural defects or injuries.

But surgery isn't always the answer — at least not all by itself. One retired man was still suffering miserably despite seven back surgeries, including the insertion of a steel plate in his neck, before he found out about CMO. He also had numbness and large arthritic knobs on several of his fingers. His doctor told him they were caused by bone spurs and suggested injecting them with steroids or removing them surgically.

His back pains were so terrible he was getting nerve block injections just about every month to help control the pain. X-rays and scans revealed the existence of a large number of bone spurs. The doctors were now recommending even more surgery.

One bottle of CMO capsules reduced his pain and he has found no need for more nerve block injections. He finds that aspirin is now enough. He plans to take another set of CMO capsules to try for even better results. The knobs on his fingers are disappearing, and a throbbing in his hands that used to keep him up all night is gone completely. He no longer feels any need for surgery.

There have been thousands of similar cases, some worse, some less severe, and just about all have achieved complete or nearly complete recovery. It would take several volumes just to include a representative sample. Suffice it to say that virtually all chronic neck, back, leg, knee, and foot pain problems can be helped with CMO.

TMJ (temporomandibular joint (or jaw) disorder)

That name's such a mouthful that many people with temporal mandibular jaw disorder can't even say it without their jaws locking up. No it's not the tetanus infection called lockjaw. TMJ is a problem usually caused by jaw malformation, fracture, dislocation, or arthritis. It can even come just from biting down too hard on something.

It can vary from an occasionally bothersome jolt of pain when chewing or talking to a constant terrible pain that even inhibits normal speech. Minor cases can disappear in a few hours or a few days. Chronic TMJ can cause constant and dreadful pain that can last a lifetime.

To resolve the problem, doctors like to prescribe pain medications. Surgeons like to recommend surgery. Neurosurgeons will suggest neurosurgery. Chiropractors propose manipulative therapy. Dentists want to x-ray it. Acupuncturists want to jab you with needles. Any or all of these procedures may prove helpful. We have nothing against them.

But can you guess what usually works best for chronic TMJ? CMO, of course.

One female patient suffered from recurring TMJ pains as a result of her misaligned jaw. She had already run the gamut before finding CMO. Her chiropractor had manipulated her jaw and made it worse. A neurosurgeon had offered her pain medications. She saw a slew of dentists claiming to be TMJ specialists. One x-rayed her jaw, injected it with something, and constructed a splint for her to wear 24 hours a day. She tried acupuncture but that didn't help either.

The misalignment remained and the pains kept coming back. Then a bit of dental work on one tooth worsened the situation. She began taking a lot of Advil and a number of prescription codeine tablets daily just to maintain.

Two days after starting CMO she reported that her pains were subsiding. She now enjoys an improvement of better than 80% overall, more than enough to feel quite comfortable again.

Hers was a quick response to a very severe case. Most TMJ cases respond just as quickly. Dozens have reported 100% recoveries from the problem.

Carpal tunnel syndrome

We keep hearing repeatedly about carpal tunnel syndrome (CTS) affecting three types of people more than any others: computer operators, typists, and mail sorters. The types of repetitive motions involved end up causing lesions or inflammations that press on the median nerves of the wrists. It can be painful and incapacitating. Wrist injuries are another cause.

Conventional CTS therapies involve elevating and/or immobilizing the wrist, steroid medications, pain medications, hot or cold compresses, manipulation, and physical therapy. Billions of dollars are paid out annually in workman's compensation insurance payments. Billions more are spent by health insurance companies treating the ailment. CMO could resolve most of those cases for a tiny fraction of the cost. This is a chronic inflammatory or arthritic disorder that is most often easily remedied by CMO. Let's look at a couple of examples.

Our first case involves a man who makes his living operating computers. After years at the keyboards he developed pains in his wrists, and the fingers of both hands began locking up. Osteoarthritis was part of the problem contributing to the CTS. Within a week on CMO the pains had almost completely disappeared and the mobility in his left hand was 90% better. But mobility in his right hand improved by only 25%. Continuing CMO for another week not only got him back to normal but back on the job.

Another typical case involves a mailman who developed CTS in both hands. It's an occupational hazard that comes with the constant handling of mail. Conventional treatments didn't work and he began wrapping his wrists with elastic bandages before going to work. He wouldn't have been able to work without them.

His wrist pains disappeared shortly after starting his CMO and he was able to continue working without further discomfort.

Several months have now passed and both of these patients have continued their work free of any further symptoms.

Tennis elbow, golfer's wrist, and other sports injuries

These problems are all very similar. Tennis players absorb the shock of the ball on their racquets at the elbow, golfers get it in the wrist, and skiers absorb the shocks from their poles in their arms and shoulders.

Their knees also get a good workout. Football, hockey, and soccer players get knocked about all over.

Athletes and former athletes are among our most numerous and most contented users of CMO. Often their problems don't show up for years, but when they do they can be crippling. CMO functions very well in reversing arthritic problems caused by sports injuries. Athletes are always amazed at the relief they get with CMO.

We've said before that arthritis starts long before any symptoms appear. It starts the moment macrophages are called upon to clean up the debris of damaged cartilage. It may take years, even dozens of years, before the destruction of cartilage reaches the point where it is felt as a painful symptom.

We feel quite certain these impact related arthritic problems could be nipped in the bud if CMO were used as a preventive. Taken occasionally during an athlete's active phases CMO could alter the arthritic process very early on so as to prevent arthritis from ever developing. Unfortunately, it will take a twenty or thirty year study to confirm that theory.

Bursitis and tendinitis

The common denominator in these two ailments is the presence of calcium deposits. Both of these ailments produce very painful chronic inflammatory processes. In bursitis the inflammation occurs in the cellular membrane covering certain bony areas like the shoulders or the knees. Calcium deposits are frequently found at the sites. The inflammation associated with tendinitis is often the direct result of calcium deposits among the tendon fibres.

The pain associated with either ailment is often so severe that it restricts movement of any afflicted joints. Although CMO cannot remove the calcium deposits themselves, it often successfully controls the painful inflammatory process which then allows full use of the joint again.

Some general comments

Consulting your physician. In tens of thousands of arthritis patients, CMO has shown virtually no negative side effects. Independent laboratory tests have proved that CMO has absolutely no toxicity even at doses 500 times greater than normal. Still we suggest that anyone under the care of a physician should seek that physician's advise about adding CMO to your current therapy.

Use of other supplements or medications. Generally speaking, any medication or supplement that has proved helpful previously can be taken concurrently with CMO and need not be discontinued. There are exceptions, however, and those are various strong immunosuppressants and anti-inflammatory prescription medications which can often (but not always) slow down or block the actions of CMO. The medications that have been so identified are Methotrexate, Rheumatrex, Cloroquine, Gold Shots, Prednisone, and other steroids.

On the other hand, CMO has never been shown to interfere with the actions of any other medications or supplements. The use of vitamins, minerals, amino acids, and beneficial oil supplements is encouraged.

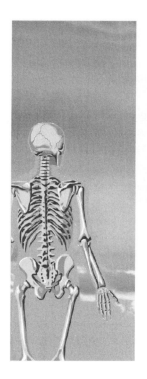

Chapter Twelve

CMO: The Ideal Program, CMO as a Preventive, and Recent Developments

CMO: The Ideal Program, CMO as a Preventive, and Recent Developments

The question comes up continuously. *If taken before any signs or symptoms of arthritis actually appear could CMO act as a preventive?*

The answer is: Probably.

And that could turn out to be true as well for many other autoimmune diseases like fibromyalgia, lupus, Crohn's disease, carpal tunnel syndrome, tendinitis, etc.

Not many doctors, therapists, or researchers give much thought to when the arthritic process actually begins in an individual. They're focused primarily on treating the disease or looking for new medications to combat it.

A person doesn't really become aware of the fact that the arthritic process has taken hold until the symptoms become rather obvious. Even the little joint pains that sometimes appear from time to time early on in the process are usually ignored. It isn't until the pain starts to come quite regularly, or until the joints begin to swell or stiffen, that the disease is recognized for what it is. By then it's too late to think of prevention. It's time to look for relief, a treatment, a cure.

However, consider this. We *can* very frequently identify the events or circumstances that may eventually bring on arthritis considerably later in life. Sometimes the symptoms of arthritis may appear quite soon, within a year or so. Sometimes they may not show up for several or even dozens of years.

Osteoarthritis

Now when it comes to osteoarthritis we're talking about events or circumstances that shock, damage, or exert excessive pressure and wear on the joints. Even normal but vigorous sports activities, not just injuries, can trigger the arthritic process. So can an automobile accident or a fall. So can working a jackhammer or regularly operating a keyboard. The former can seriously damage your joints and the latter can result in carpal tunnel syndrome.

Things like that are not hard to identify. And what would happen if someone were to take CMO shortly after such events?

Remember, we already know the arthritic process can start when macrophages encounter damaged or unhealthy cartilage and start their cleanup job, and then report their activities back to the Memory T-cells that program autoimmune processes. Well, there it is, the beginning of the autoimmune process that can result in arthritis sometime sooner or later.

Please note that we say *can*, not *will*, because it may be that every such event does not trigger the autoimmune arthritic process. But we well know that the great majority of athletes, jackhammer operators, and joint trauma victims do eventually develop arthritis in the affected joints. We see or hear from them every day.

But could CMO have nipped it in the bud? The answer is, as before, *probably*. There's very likely a matter of timing involved. If a course of CMO capsules were taken only once before the whole macrophage cleanup action was completed, then the ongoing cleanup process would continue to affect the Memory T-cells and the autoimmune arthritic process would probably still be triggered.

But if the course of CMO capsules were taken after the whole macrophage cleanup process was completed, then it would probably correct the existing Memory T-cell programming and halt the arthritic process before it ever reached a stage where any symptoms would ever become evident. That would be true, of course, only if their were no additional traumas or damage to the areas.

On the other hand, for those who suffer repeated joint trauma, it is likely that taking CMO a couple times a year could well prevent arthritis from ever occurring. Or it could be taken after the events are no longer likely to occur - like retiring from football or changing jobs.

Rheumatoid arthritis

It would be more difficult to identify the events or circumstances that might trigger the autoimmune process for rheumatoid arthritis. The macrophage involvement is identical, of course.

So what signs would you look for? It's well known that rheumatic fever often results in rheumatoid arthritis. We also know that aching joints are often present during several types of flu infections. Nobody seems to have established any connection between the flu and any subsequent appearance of rheumatoid arthritis. But then, I don't think anybody has investigated that possible connection.

Actually, nobody seems to know what triggers the autoimmune arthritic process so we don't know what events or circumstances to look for. In the medical dictionaries "rheumatoid arthritis" is simply defined as an inflammation of the joint that causes changes in the connective tissue. Cause unknown.

Our best advice to anyone thinking of CMO as a preventive for rheumatoid arthritis is to be suspicious of any joint pain.

Other forms of arthritis, other diseases

Reactive arthritis is a label that just generally refers to any kind of joint inflammation resulting from sensitivity to some particular disease or substance. Psoriatic arthritis is one of those. People with psoriasis often develop arthritis. As a probable preventive for this type of arthritis, CMO would best be taken at the very first signs of psoriasis. It has even helped control the skin disease itself.

A few university investigations seems to have determined that there is a small segment of the population whose arthritis is caused by food sensitivities - mostly to wheat, corn, or milk products. If cutting one or more of those food products out of a diet tends to relieve arthritis symptoms even a little, then it may possibly be the source of that reactive arthritis. It may be necessary to eliminate the trigger foods permanently. Otherwise, continued use would keep triggering the process anew.

The same may be true for certain substances like dust or pollen or chemicals or vapours.

As for chronic or degenerative diseases (like fibromyalgia, lupus, scleroderma, etc), these often appear in other family members. Anyone with a family history of such ailments may do well to be on the alert for the slightest sign if they care to use CMO as a preventive.

Preventive studies

There are no studies currently under way. Any such study would be an enormous project and would have to involve large numbers of subjects before any significant statistics could be evaluated.

It would be most difficult to interpret the results and would require decades to complete. And just how could it be determined if test subjects would have developed arthritis if they had not taken CMO? There are virtually no standard statistics available for comparison.

So what about the question, "*If taken before any signs or symptoms of arthritis actually appear, could CMO act as a preventive?*"

Theoretically, yes, absolutely! It would be better for athletes to take CMO a couple times a year to deal with the mis-programmed T-cells immediately and never let the joint trauma develop into severe arthritis. Ditto for anyone regularly playing sport, subject to joint trauma or for anyone with repetitive motion occupations, like jackhammer operators and typists.

In theory, yes, it would be better for anyone with joint pain from the flu or with a family history of chronic or degenerative diseases to take CMO once or twice a year as a preventive.

In practice, we don't yet know. It won't be until a couple dozen years have passed with several hundred people having tried it that way before we know for certain. A few concerned and vulnerable people have already begun. If you do, too, we'd like to hear from you.

Prevention & Therapy - New Discoveries

Since the publication of the first version of this book, we've had the joy of knowing that over 100,000 arthritis sufferers have substantially benefited by taking certified CMO in its various approved formulations. CMO is often combined with other nutritional substances that contribute additional benefits to its healing effects, such as sea cucumber, DL-phenylalanine, and glucosamine sulphate. In this chapter, I will share with you some of these amazing new health discoveries.

First of all, the success rates of curing arthritis and other disorders using CMO continue to be astonishing. One authorized distributor of certified CMO reports a 96% customer satisfaction rate. This high level of customer satisfaction duplicates the success rate of the original study conducted by the San Diego Clinic (now renamed San Diego International Immunological Center after considerable expansion of its research efforts). Since the purpose of the original study was to determine the beneficial health effects of CMO only on arthritis, subjects with only arthritis as their sole medical complaint were accepted for the study. Additionally, individuals who had been or were currently taking potent immunosuppressants, including high doses of steroids, were also deemed to be unsuitable as subjects. This pre-selection is normal practice in medical trials. No one expected the success rates of CMO formulations for the general public use to be more than about 70%, especially as people would be taking CMO without the benefit of clinical supervision. Yet, remarkably, success rates in the field have almost always exceeded our expectation.

The clinic's research and the practical experiences of working with thousands of patients has revealed a great deal more about arthritis and other autoimmune diseases than was previously known. We have also discovered much about the arthritic and autoimmune processes from our own continuing research, as well as the research of my colleagues. This new knowledge has prompted expansion of some of my approaches to CMO treatment programs.

When we began our CMO research, we did so with the intent of attaining remission against the autoimmune processes of arthritis. That was our focus. However it was not long after

CMO was being utilized by physicians and other medical professionals in their practices, that I began receiving reports of various benefits for many other autoimmune and chronic inflammatory conditions. It was only then that I realized that CMO was a universal-autoimmune immunomodulator. That is what launched new research that led to a more complete understanding of memory T-cell function and how the autoimmune processes cause a variety of degenerative diseases. (See Chapter 1 for information on memory T-cell function.)

Although CMO routinely succeeds in affecting a person's entire memory T-cell population, and halting the destructive autoimmune disease process, I still found a number of patients whose symptoms began to return after some length of time. Sometimes it was just a matter of a few weeks or a few months, and sometimes it took a year or more.

The excepts from the following letter illustrate these types of recurrences:

Dear Dr. Sands,

Thanks so much for the articles and testimonials. I am a true believer myself because it worked so well for me. I can't thank you enough for agreeing to make this injectable [CMO] for me and my friend. It means a lot.

Again thank you from the bottom of my heart. CMO has really saved my life. I didn't think I could ever live free of pain, but CMO changed all that and more. I don't take Prozac any longer, nor do I take Advil [up to 10 a day before]...

I think your other research is really fascinating. I used to think I had Parkinson's or MS or something because I would shake so much, but Prozac fixed that. And CMO fixed whatever it was permanently so I don't need Prozac.

I do need tune-ups, about every 3-4 months or when I go through a stressful period. But CMO takes care of whatever is wrong. I can't say enough about how great it is, and I can't thank you enough for taking the time to pursue CMO to a point where it's available to all people.

Thanks again. May God bless you in every way,

Micky C., Colorado

My new research and understanding of how easily and frequently autoimmune processes are started, lead me to the explanation of these recurrences. *Virtually any infection, trauma, disease, or environmental factor can trigger an autoimmune response.* We are faced with these exposure events nearly every day. Often the body deals with these events in an effective manner that does not trigger a destructive autoimmune process. Sometimes a new autoimmune response is triggered and simply withers away. Sometimes it lingers and goes unnoticed, but then it almost always develops into a troublesome or crippling ailment. This process may happen quickly or it may take months or years before it develops tormenting symptoms.

These autoimmune hiccups abound in our modern environment so often that it has prompted me to develop what I consider to be a very valuable maintenance and preventive treatment program. Since CMO has now proved to be a universal-immunomodulator, this new program should prove effective against a very large number of ailments with autoimmune factors. Such ailments include fibromyalgia, lupus, sarcoidosis, scleroderma, multiple sclerosis, emphysema, asthma, some allergies, prostatitis, juvenile diabetes, diabetes, psoriasis, macular degeneration, tendinitis, sciatica, and others - as well as all forms of arthritis.

But before I explain this new CMO preventive/maintenance program, let's have a look at some of the substances involved. I have found sea cucumber, DLPA, and glucosamine to be particularly beneficial and completely compatible with using CMO.

Sea Cucumber

Let's first have a look at sea cucumber, an ancient therapeutic agent used for thousands of years in Chinese medicine. Numerous modem scientific research studies show that sea cucumber helps to control inflammatory processes in the body. As a result, sea cucumber often provides relief of the inflammation associated with rheumatoid and osteoarthritis, tendinitis, sports injuries, sprains, and joint pains, as well as other inflammatory diseases. One study found that it also improved the body's overall resistance to stress.

Sea cucumber works by helping to regulate biochemical substances known as prostaglandins which are involved in inflammatory processes. It also contains chondroitin which the body finds valuable to help produce new joint cartilage, and it is a good source of lubricating compounds that are found in the joints and joint fluids. The famous nutritionist Earl Mindell describes sea cucumber as *"an even more potent anti-inflammatory agent than hydrocortisone."* The benefits of sea cucumber for most arthritis patients has even been proved in medical studies. It has been approved by the Australian Department of Health as an effective treatment for arthritis and is widely used in the Orient and Europe for that purpose.

An analysis of dried sea cucumber reveals that it is about 80% protein. Other substances found are chondroitin sulphate, and the beneficial minerals boron, calcium, chromium, copper, iodine, iron, magnesium, manganese, silicon, and zinc. Good mineral balance in the body has always been recognized as being valuable for joint health. The safety and the effectiveness of sea cucumber's therapeutic effects has been demonstrated over thousands of years in practical application, as well as now by modern laboratory testing and clinical trials. Though rare, a few sensitive persons have developed a minor rash from its use.

More evidence of the beneficial effects of the combination of CMO and sea cucumber has been provided by a study conducted by Dr Alan Edwards in England. He reports on a small trial with fibromyalgia suffers which showed improvement for the majority after only 4 weeks use of this combination. Importantly, those that improved showed a very promising improvement, whilst those that did not, had hardly any positive impact at all, perhaps because they failed to absorb the nutrients involved. At the time writing this report is awaiting publication in a respected journal, currently scheduled for the middle of this year.

DL-phenylalanine (DLPA)

DLPA (DL-phenylalanine) is a very interesting substance that reduces pain quickly and effectively. It can help patients promptly gain a satisfying level of comfort while waiting for the long-lasting benefits of CMO to take effect. In the body endorphins are the natural substances produced to control the transmission of pain signals. Although they are non-narcotic, endorphins can be thought of as a sort of natural morphine.

DLPA prevents the normal hasty destruction of endorphins and thus inhibits the transmission of pain signals. It works by inhibiting the enzymes that break down endorphins, which results in extending their beneficial effects for a much longer time. In some people, DLPA sometimes acts as a mood enhancer as well.

L-phenylalanine and D-phenylalanine are natural amino acid substances commonly found in many protein foods. DL-phenylalanine is a combination of the two. Most people enjoy very prompt pain relief with DLPA and experience no negative side effects. It is safe and effective, gentle on the stomach, and not habit-forming. And it does not contribute through joint cartilage deterioration as do aspirin and other NSAIDS.

However take note that although not common, some people experience headaches or nausea from taking DLPA. People with high blood pressure, women who are pregnant or lactating, persons with psychoses, those suffering from malignant melanoma, those with phenylketonuria, or those with any sensitivity to phenylalanine should consult their physician before taking DLPA containing products. Taking DLPA with MAO or tricyclic antidepressants can lead to dangerously high blood pressure.

Glucosamine Sulphate

Glucosamine is a nutritional marvel of medical science. Glucosamine has received a great deal of attention over the past few years because of its benefits for rebuilding cartilage and connective tissue that has been destroyed as a result of the arthritic process, from aging, or physical trauma damage. Its benefits have eased the suffering of millions around the world. Although touted as a cure, it is not. Glucosamine does not stop or slow down autoimmune attacks against the joints. Nevertheless, it is of enormous value because it promotes the production of special biochemicals called proteoglycans, which are water-retaining molecules that are the building blocks of collagen, cartilage, and connective tissue. Unfortunately, over the long run arthritis often destroys cartilage faster than the body can replace it even with the help of glucosamine supplements. Fortunately CMO can, and usually does, halt the arthritic process itself. Glucosamine and CMO support each other's benefits and work together superbly.

Once CMO has stopped the arthritic process, and halted the continuing destruction of cartilage, the body is then free to build up cartilage to normal levels again. But cartilage production is normally a very slow process. Glucosamine sulphate can speed up cartilage replacement dramatically. Ample cartilage levels are necessary to regain normal joint function and eliminate joint pain. Obviously cartilage replacement cannot be accomplished in an instant.

Scientific studies clearly demonstrate that it takes a few weeks for glucosamine to produce noticeable results. For example, a double-blind clinical study involving 178 patients in Beijing with osteoarthritis of the knees compared the effects of glucosamine with ibuprofen. Although both groups experienced improvements, the glucosamine provided a stronger effect, and was better tolerated than ibuprofen. A general summary of several studies indicates that glucosamine gradually reduces joint pain and tenderness while improving ease of movement.

Another study, reported in the prestigious British medical journal, *The Lancet* in January 2001 found that glucosamine sulphate used for long term did appear to prevent changes in joint structure and significantly improve symptoms of osteoarthritis. This was three year, double blind study.

In contrast, another medical study indicated that older, heavier people with severe arthritis may not respond as well to glucosamine therapy. Since some studies assert that as people age they lose the ability to manufacture sufficient levels of glucosamine, it may be even more important for older people to take glucosamine regularly as part of a maintenance therapy.

Other glucosamine medical studies indicated that patients taking nonsteroidal anti-inflammatory prescription drugs (NSAIDS) were able to comfortably cut their dosages to one-third or one-half of their customary amounts. Clinical trials have proved that aspirin and other NSAIDS inhibit cartilage repair, and accelerate cartilage destruction. Although they help relieve pain they contribute to the worsening of arthritis.

Glucosamine is needed in the formation of a wide variety of body structures including tendons, ligaments, vertebral disks, synovial fluid, cell membranes, blood vessels, skin, organs, nails, hair, bone, and the connective tissues which literally fill in gaps all over our body. Studies conducted on humans taking daily dosages of glucosamine between 500mg to 1,500mg per day have demonstrated the ability of dietary glucosamine to stimulate the production of connective tissue and its repair. Some of the benefits reported from these clinical studies include:

- Improved joint structure and function.
- Maintenance of cartilage tissue.
- Repair of worn and damaged connective tissues in joints.
- Growth of cartilage, collagen, skin tissue, ligaments, and other connective tissues.
- Promotion of the manufacture of the body's natural joint lubricant.
- Improved skin appearance and thickness.

Connective tissues are chiefly made of collagen, a tough stringy protein. Collagen is a major tissue in the human body, making up almost 30% of total body protein content. The building and rebuilding of collagen in the body is a constant process. During periods of stress, exercise, or wear the demand for the building blocks of collagen and proteoglycans increases. More glucosamine in needed to keep up with this demand. The body makes glucosamine from glucose, but there are no significant food sources of glucosamine. Taking supplemental glucosamine stimulates the production of the collagen needed to make connective tissue.

Glucosamine sulphate has been used in most clinical studies all over the world. It has a long history of safe and effective use by humans; contains a beneficial sulphur molecule; is backed by detailed clinical research on thousands of human subjects; and its absorption and bioavailability are confirmed. Some other forms of glucosamine may be inferior, but recent research indicates that glucosamine HCl is also effective. Some scientists believe that glucosamine sulphate has added benefits because it also supplies the body with sulphur, which is an element that is used in connective tissue formation.

There are indications that long-term glucosamine use may sometimes affect blood sugar control in diabetic patients. Diabetics should monitor blood sugar levels more frequently while taking glucosamine. People with peptic ulcers should take glucosamine sulphate with foods. Glucosamine may also reduce the effectiveness of diuretics.

Rethinking arthritis therapy

Yes, CMO can halt the arthritic and other autoimmune processes as it reaches and affects all the responsible memory T-cells in the body at the time. But, as I mentioned earlier in this chapter, we are constantly being exposed to factors that can trigger new autoimmune processes nearly every day. It makes good sense to me that taking CMO at regular intervals can stop these processes before they can even began to do any damage. That's a million times better and easier than trying to correct a serious problem after it develops.

This would be about as true for an office worker or a housewife as it would be for a football player or a jackhammer operator. The minor bumps and infections experienced by a clerk are almost as likely to start an arthritic process as the severe jolts experienced by hockey players. That is pretty well confirmed by the number of people who develop arthritis as they grow older. Nearly half of the entire U.S. population has developed arthritis by the time they reach the age of 65. Actually the arthritic process is most likely to have started many years before and have been further aggravated by continuing minor events and wear and tear as time passed. They weren't all hockey players. Doesn't it make sense to stop the process long before it begins to ruin your joints? And doesn't it make sense to give your body all the help you can to fix any damage that has already occurred? As previously explained, it usually takes a very long time for joints and surrounding tissues to deteriorate to the point where it becomes noticeable. It takes even longer before any symptoms of pain or inflammation appear. The concept of keeping your body supplied with the nutrients it needs for good joint and connective tissue health is very sound and mandatory for everyone.

An ideal program

Even though CMO halts autoimmune inflammatory processes, it has no direct anti-inflammatory action of its own. Even though it stops autoimmune attacks at their source (the memory T-cells), and allows the regeneration of cartilage to build up undisturbed, CMO provides no nutrients to encourage it. Combining CMO with sea cucumber would then provide more immediate anti-inflammatory action as well as some nutrients to help rebuild cartilage and encourage the production of synovial fluid for the lubrication of the joints. Adding 100 milligrams of sea cucumber extract to the time-tested dosage program using 385 milligrams of certified CMO per capsule, taking two capsules each morning and evening, a total of 4 capsules per day, is proven to be of great benefit in my clinical experience.

This course of nutritional therapy should then be followed up by taking a dosage of 400 to 750 milligrams of timed-release glucosamine sulphate twice a day, and 200 to 500 milligrams of DLPA twice a day. This will provide the nutrients needed to repair and maintain good joint health and continuing comfort. Because glucosamine is excreted from the body so very quickly, using a newly developed, proprietary sustained release version is far more effective because it maintains stable blood glucosamine levels throughout the day and night. That's far better than the stop-start routine of ordinary glucosamine products.

I recommend the following as an ideal program for nutritional therapy of an existing condition, maintenance from a relapse and prevention against developing an ailment. My recommendation is borne out the experience of thousands taking CMO in the past few years.

Take the CMO for an initial several week period to stop the destructive autoimmune process. Follow this up with longer term taking of the timed-release glucosamine and DLPA in the dosages previously mentioned and sea cucumber extracts to suit. This is designed to encourage repair work. You may then consider taking "refresher" courses of CMO in periods varying from every few months to eighteen or more months, depending on your individual circumstances and your environment. This is designed to kick-start your improvement as well as act as a preventive.

Index

Index

F

fatty acid waxes *117*

FDA *117*

fibromyalgia *23, 77, 126, 130, 163*

flu *18, 55*

food sensitivities *157*

G

glucosamine sulphate *164*

glucosamines *11*

goats *58, 95*

Gold Shots *152*

golfer's wrist *150*

Grave's disease *24*

H

hamsters *58, 95*

headaches *144*

    cluster *144*

    migraine *144*

    tension *144*

    vascular *144*

Herxheimer *29*

high blood pressure *145*

Hoffman, Felix *32*

horses *58, 95*

Hunt, Dr. Douglas *12, 32, 59, 74*

hypertension *145, 146*

I

immunomodulator *41, 48*

immunosuppressant *121, 152*

inflammation *16, 17, 19, 51*

irritable bowel *139*

irritable bowel syndrome *23*